The Complete

FONDUE

Menu and Party Book

Books by Beatrice A. Ojakangas

GOURMET COOKING FOR TWO

THE FINNISH COOK BOOK

The Complete

FONDUE

Menu and Party Book

BEATRICE A. OJAKANGAS

Illustrations by Margery Kronengold

Crown Publishers, Inc. ❀ New York

Special thanks go to Cathy and Greg for their
assistance in preparing the manuscript and
index. Further thanks to my husband, Dick,
who did most of the critical tasting, and
to Susanne, whose "assistance" kept progress
behind schedule

Library of Congress Catalog Card Number: 73-185070
Manufactured in the United States of America
Published simultaneously in Canada by
General Publishing Company Limited
Designed by Margery Kronengold

Contents

1677762

The Complete
FONDUE
Menu and Party Book

Fondue Lore

☀ When I first heard about fondue, some fourteen years ago, it was from our Finnish pediatrician who had just visited Switzerland. He exclaimed ecstatically about that "Vonderful Sviss Seese Diss" that he had enjoyed in that country. Being the kind of warm and friendly person he is, the greatest delight of this "seese diss" was the feeling of friendship that went along with it.

Fondues have come a long way since then. Now it's almost a household word. "Almost everybody gets a fondue pot as a wedding gift these days!" exclaimed a young bride-to-be who was contemplating buying a pot and then decided against it.

But there are many who still ask, "What *is* fondue?"

The word "fondue" comes from the French word "fondre" which means "to melt." Therefore, a true fondue is a dish of

1

something that has been melted. It's served as a dunk or a dip. But according to historical lore the dish goes back to the days when the meal for the whole family was cooked in one pot which was placed in the middle of the table for consumption. But there were many kinds of dishes prepared this way—porridges, gruels, potato and cheese dishes—because it was both simple to serve and expedient to prepare. The participants used spoons, pieces of bread, or boiled potatoes to scoop up some of the contents of the pot. The meal continued as long as the head of the household was eating. When he finished, everybody else stopped eating too.

Many of the elements of the communal pot are preserved with the fondue style of eating. Although we do offer dishes for individual diners and even add other dishes to the menu, basically the feeling of togetherness is preserved when fondue is enjoyed with family and friends. In a way, to partake of fondue is a test of sensitivity and interpersonal relationships.

What, then, is fondue?

Well, we know that cheese fondue originated in Switzerland. We also know that cheese, bread, and wine are peasant staples of that country. It isn't hard to figure out that some imaginative Swiss cook had some choices to make when facing those three basics. She could either slice the cheese, serve it on bread, and drink the wine (which undoubtedly was done) or for the sake of variety she could melt the cheese into the wine and eat the mixture with bread (perhaps with more wine).

If the Swiss were inventive enough to use three elements in such a creative manner, why not elaborate and expand on the idea? For the melting medium there are other cheeses available to us and many foods that substitute well for bread to dunk into the resulting mixture. So, in this book we will vary the theme of fondue a bit. We'll tell you what else to serve with it to complete the meal (it's up to you whether you *want* anything else with the fondue, but we'll make the suggestions. Fair enough?)

But the question arises, "What about beef fondue?" Why is it called a fondue even though nothing is melted in anything? I don't really know, but there is a common "action" in the method of eating (dipping in the pot), and there's a common feeling about the eating (togetherness). Probably the common activity of dipping relates the two fondues, Cheese Fondue or *Fondue Neufchâteloise* and Beef Fondue or *Fondue Bourguignonne.*

But again, how did Beef Fondue originate?

Once upon a time there was a portly Swiss fellow who loved his cheese fondue so much that he had to have it almost every day. As much as the fondue, he loved the company he kept while he enjoyed the fondue, for it was an old tradition that whoever drops his cube of bread into the sauce gets to kiss the pretty girls to his right and to his left.

Then one day this portly Swiss fellow went to the doctor for his annual checkup. The doctor took one look at him and said, "No more fondue for you! No cheese. No bread. And no more wine." How his plump patient wept! "No more pretty Swiss girls to my right and to my left!"

The portly Swiss fellow grew very depressed and withdrawn, until finally he decided to take a trip to lift him from his state of gloom. He went to the south of France and nobody saw him for a long time. Everybody speculated as to what could have become of the once jolly fellow who was expelled from the delights of fondue. Then one day he returned to Switzerland full of his old robust joy and high spirits. They all marveled at how well he looked, and couldn't imagine what he found that took the place of his beloved cheese fondue.

That night he invited all his friends and the pretty Swiss girls to his house. He ordered them not to snoop in the kitchen while he produced his new invention.

Voilà! Fondue Bourguignonne! The once-portly Swiss fellow explained that after much thought and soul-searching, he decided it was the dipping in the pot and the friends that he missed the most. And in the days of his wanderings in the south of France he meditated heavily and finally came up with an answer.

He produced a pot of bubbling oil along with bowls of tender beef. He could enjoy the delights of the fondue again. Now, when he dropped his meat into the oil, he could kiss the pretty girls to his right and to his left.

The world is so much richer for his invention. Because this Swiss was so creative and came up with a new variety of fondue, he certainly would not object if we embroider the theme a bit. We cook other things in oil besides beef. Sometimes we cook things in broth instead of oil, and sometimes we're so creative we're not sure what we're cooking, but we *are* dipping out of the pot. I really don't think that our portly Swiss fellow would mind at all. Do you?

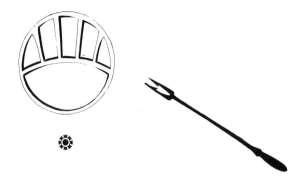

An Introduction to Serving Fondue

☀ Why serve fondue? That's a personal question with an interpersonal answer. We don't serve it just because "it's the thing to do." We do serve it because we have some very good friends and we wish to dine with them. There are more reasons, too.

Basically people like to serve fondue because it's an informal, unpretentious way to entertain. It leaves the hostess free from the kitchen because the important cooking is really done at the table by the guests.

Fondue is relaxing. You are compelled to eat slowly; therefore it is better for your health. Fondue is thoughtful. For guests who are watching their diet, it is easy to gauge what you eat without being conspicuous about it.

One of my favorite reasons for serving fondue is that there's plenty of time for good conversation. Fondue breaks the ice somehow and allows your guests to be themselves. Sometimes the topic of conversation is serious and thoughtful and it can swing in a split second to something uproariously funny. That's what *I* like about fondue.

Once you're hooked on serving fondues, you may wish for some variety. And that's what this book is about: to answer questions and provide menus and recipes and ideas for expanding the fondue theme.

What to serve with fondue is sometimes a tough question when you don't know much about fondue in the first place. We'll provide menus and recipes for additional dishes to give you specific ideas about what you may serve with what. We'll try to warn you of special timing (such as when you can or should make something the day before). You may have better ideas, or have other preferences, or you may want to skip a certain dish altogether. That's fine. With a meat fondue you may want to serve side dishes to "stretch" the fondue meat. Then again, you may not. Sometimes it's interesting and exciting to have flavor variety within the meal. That's why there are accompanying dishes suggested with the fondues.

Some hostesses are afraid of serving too little or that somebody may not like something and that person go hungry. These cooks often serve staggering quantities. That's not necessary, although I can appreciate their concern. Perhaps the greatest hostess-damage ever was captured by a cartoon I saw years ago that depicted a man heading straight for the refrigerator after getting home from a dinner party. Good cooks *do* fear that. But they shouldn't. Many more cartoons have been sketched of the man drinking Alka-Seltzer through the night after a heavy meal. Hostesses should avoid that.

With fondue, however, it is rare that anybody leaves the table hungry. Fondue is filling all by itself because it's eaten over a long period of time and slowly. This means that fondue menus can be the starkest examples of simplicity. Just the basic fondue and a beverage is totally adequate. A simple salad can put a person beyond the bursting point (though I prefer to serve a salad for the texture contrast in the menu).

The menus in this book feature complete meals for two important reasons: (1) to suggest accompaniments that add complementary textures and flavors to your meal, if you wish to serve with flair, and (2) to show that fondues are not so self-centered that they cannot share the limelight and help enhance other foods.

How do you serve a fondue? Part of the answer lies just in the paraphernalia (next chapter). Within each menu are specific suggestions if the menu varies from the basic procedure at all. To serve fondue is simple. You put the fondue pot (cheese or bubbling oil for beef) in the center of the table. For cheese fondue, guests spear a chunk of bread and dunk it into the cheese sauce, then eat it. For beef fondue they spear a cube of beef and cook it in the oil, eating it with sauces that you provide to complement the flavor.

Setting the table. Place the fondue pot on its burner in the center of the table. I prefer to preheat the oil for beef fondue in the kitchen ahead of time and transfer it to the table just before we all sit down to eat. With cheese fondue I do the same thing—I make the fondue in the kitchen and transfer it onto a burner just before we sit down. Plan on two to six persons per fondue pot. No more. Set the table (round is best) with fondue plates (for beef fondue you use the kind with indentations for sauces). Or, if you don't have the special plates, any kind will do. For cheese fondues, use regular plates that are informal, colorful, gay. Set flatware as you always do. I like to lay the fondue fork (the funny-looking kind with sharp spearlike points) across the plate. There's really no rule. Actually, you can use ordinary forks with a cheese type fondue. But when you're cooking beef or meat in oil a regular fork would get too hot to handle. That's why steel fondue forks are designed with wooden handles. Use mugs for coffee or tea, informal glasses for wine.

In general, when setting your table for fondue, try to make it as colorful, informal, and gay as you can.

✺

Fondue Paraphernalia

✺ So now you're sold on fondue. You've been eying those pretty pots and all those fascinating dishes and forks that belong to fondue. Perhaps you received some of the equipment as a gift—for wedding, anniversary, Christmas, or whatever. But you haven't yet figured these utensils out.

Before you rush out to buy all kinds of paraphernalia, *hold it!* The market is flooded with all kinds of fondue pots. Some are cheap. Others are expensive. Some are made of copper or other metals or pottery and come in pretty colors. Some are just not worth buying.

There are two classic types of fondue pots. One is used basically for beef and the other for cheese.

Beef fondue pots are made of metal and have a potbellied shape. There's a reason for the funny shape. The pot is to be filled only about half full of oil for cooking. Therefore, the surface of the oil loses less heat to the air because the top of the pot slants in protectively. Secondly, the problem of the oil sizzling and splashing and causing bad burns is diminished. And, because you rest your fork with the meat speared on the tip in the pot for a few minutes to cook, you need to have the upper rim of the pot high enough and narrow enough to support the fork.

Beef fondue pots are usually made of copper, enameled metal, or stainless steel. You should be careful to get a sturdy one because the lightweight (and cheaper) ones can be dangerous. The handles can come loose and you can very easily spill hot oil if you have to lift the pot for any reason. Heavier pots distribute the heat evenly, whereas lightweight ones will create a hot spot. It is also possible for the oil to get so hot in this one spot that it can burst into flames. Heavier pots are much safer, sturdier, and, alas, more expensive.

In selecting one of those expensive beef fondue pots, the difference is mainly esthetic. Copper is beautiful. It should be lined with stainless steel or tin like most good copper cookware. Keeping copper gleaming is *not* an esthetic job, especially if you fondue a lot. My favorite is a Norwegian fondue pot made of enameled metal that is very heavy and sturdy.

Cheese type fondue pots are another story. You don't see them in such profusion on the market, but the different shape and construction materials have a purpose, too. Cheese fondue pots have a wide, open top, a capacity of about one and one-half quarts, and usually are made of heatproof crockery. Any wide heavy casserole with a handle will do for cheese fondue if it is thick enough so that the cheese will not burn in one spot. I have two heavy enameled cast-iron pots with handles that work well. Cheese fondue cannot take the high and concentrated heat required to keep oil hot in the beef type fondue pots; the heat must be distributed gently. A heavy pot will do this. A beef fondue pot won't work.

There is one exception to this rule: that is with the electric fondue pots where you can control the heat very accurately. But, for this control you sacrifice the beauty and romance of the flame.

Dessert fondues, the real "youngsters" in the fondue family,

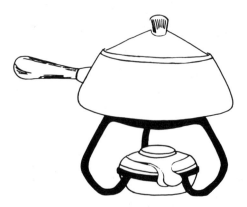

The Beef Fondue Pot

The beef fondue pot is made of metal, stainless steel, or copper, to transmit heat quickly and intensely. Handle is usually of wood. When buying this type of pot, check to see that the handle will not loosen easily, causing dangerous spilling of hot oil. Top opening is relatively small to minimize splattering. Beef fondue pots usually have a lid. The alcohol burner is the most popular type. This has a lid to smother the flame and a handle that adjusts the amount of air that feeds the flame for proper heat control.

The Cheese Fondue Pot (Caquelon)

The cheese fondue pot is usually made of fireproof pottery or heavy cast aluminum coated with enamel, or of a heavy glasslike material. The most important feature is that it disperses heat evenly over the bottom of the pot so as not to burn the cheese fondue. Note the wide-open top. The burner in this illustration is the type that burns denatured alcohol. It has a lid to smother the flame and a handle to adjust the heat.

must be heated gently. For them, use a heavy crockery flameproof pot and a *very* low flame. In fact, an efficient candle is about ideal. Since most dessert fondues are quite sweet, the recipes produce no more than two cups of the fondue at the most, which is about half the capacity of a cheese fondue. Therefore, the pot you choose for a dessert fondue should be smaller than that for a cheese fondue.

Burners on the fondue pots vary in style as well as in the fuel they're designed to burn. My favorite is the type that burns denatured alcohol. It's also the most common. Denatured alcohol goes into burners that have a white cotton material inside the cavity. You control the heat by opening or closing the holes on the movable cap that has a handle. Denatured alcohol is inexpensive and can be bought by the gallon at paint stores.

Lately I've noticed denatured alcohol specially bottled and labeled for fondue. It's much more expensive, of course.

The Chocolate Fondue Pot

The chocolate fondue pot generally has a capacity of one to one and a half cups. The pot is crockery or otherwise nonmetallic. Since heat source must be low, a candle is adequate.

The second most popular type of burner takes a can of sterno. This is more costly to use, and it works as well. Most of the sterno burners have a little cover that you turn to control the heat.

Butane burners are featured on some of the most expensive pots. They're beautiful, and allow very close control of the heat, almost like the flame on a gas range. And, of course, electric fondue pots offer the same precise control of the heat. My only objection to the electric fondue pot is the cord. Somehow it seems too modern. Someone should invent a fondue table with a hole in the center for the fondue pot and an electrical outlet under the table.

Fondue forks are really necessary only for beef fondue or when you're cooking in hot oil. The handles are wooden so they won't get hot, and the prongs are very sharp and pointed to spear the

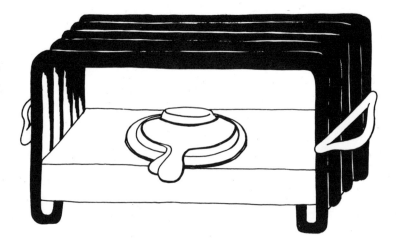

The Alcohol Burner

This is one of many types available on the market that can serve any kind of fondue pot. It is practical to buy just one burner to use for both beef and cheese fondue pots. Look for one that is easy to keep clean and is sturdy enough to avoid the possibility of the pot's tipping or spilling. The alcohol burner uses denatured alcohol, has a lid to smother the flame, and can be adjusted to control heat.

meat securely. You can buy them in many places, and the cost ranges from four for a dollar to more than two dollars each. Again, although you pay more for better quality, they last longer.

For cheese fondue use regular dinner forks, dip and eat with the same one, but if this bothers you, then you *could* provide two forks. Use one fork for dipping and the other for eating.

Those divided fondue plates you see everywhere are great fun to have when you're serving a beef fondue with sauces. You're supposed to put different sauces into the divisions. You *can* get by without fondue plates and just be messy and spoon the sauces right onto your dinner plate. For a very runny sauce such as a teriyaki, you'd have to provide little soufflé cups. Paper ones are

The Fondue Plate
Fondue plates may have four or five separations for sauces and are available in pottery, plastic, or china in many attractive colors.

The Fondue Fork
Beef fondue forks are made of metal. The handle is usually wooden to provide insulation from the heat of the bubbling oil. The fork tines have very sharp points that pierce through the meat and hooks to secure meat as it cooks. The better the quality of the fondue fork, the heavier and sturdier it will be—and the more expensive.

fine. Large bottle caps would work fine, too. Fondue is very informal.

The table setting should be casual. Forget the crystal and china (we don't own any, anyway), and use pottery, stainless flatware, mugs for coffee, big fat candles for atmosphere. For wine, use pottery mugs, Oriental teacups, or some of those clear plastic semidisposable glasses. Colorful place mats, colorful table runners, or no tablecloth at all are other ways to get a rustic, informal effect. Checked gingham, torn into squares, or red farmer handkerchiefs make colorful and informal napkins.

The Tempura Pan and Alcohol Burner

This side view shows that the tempura pan is shallow, with a two- to three-inch "beach" around the edge. It has a rack that fits on the side of the pan for draining the tempura morsels. Tempura pans are relatively inexpensive and do not come with their own burners. Illustrated is a sturdy burner that is suitable for all kinds of fondue because it is adjustable.

Just remember that fondue is relaxed, fun, friendly, casual. It's for friends and people you want to know better. Don't rush out and buy all kinds of paraphernalia: get the basics, borrow what you can (we're forever borrowing fondue forks). Improvise. Make do. Learn to "know" fondue before you stock up on things. Consider renting fondue pots if you can't borrow them. Just remember always to return borrowed items in as good condition as you received them.

The Oriental Firepot

The Oriental firepot is usually made of brass. A lid covers the moat, which holds the hot broth used for cooking meat and vegetables. The tall chimney in the center of the pot leads down to the chamber where hot charcoal briquettes are placed to keep the broth hot.

A Beef Fondue Party for Four Close Friends

✹ We could call this "getting your feet wet," if it's your first attempt. Fondue is about the easiest thing to serve once you get the hang of it. Anything new is scary the first time, especially if you're timid about cooking for guests. So try it out the first time with only four people. You'll discover to your great delight that you're free from kitchen drudgery and actually have time for good conversation with your guests once you sit down to eat. Each person cooks his own meat, piece by piece. This takes lots of time. You eat slowly and leisurely, and that's better for your health.

When you invite your friends, tell them this is a "first." Most people are very helpful and kind when you level with them. In fact, this is almost always a way to put people at ease and transfer any nervous feeling into one of excitement and adventure. If they've had fondue before, they're glad to offer advice. Accept it willingly. If they've never had fondue before, you're discovering it together.

Shopping for fondue is simple. Buy the meat the day you plan to serve it. Boneless beef sirloin or tenderloin is best. At home you cut it up, put it in a bowl, and it's ready. Check the menu and recipes for other things you'll need. Make a list and do your shopping. Don't forget oil for the pot and denatured alcohol or sterno, depending on the type of burner you're using.

You may wish to omit things from the following menu—such as the Rice Pilaf with Mushrooms and one of the sauces.

✿

Fondue Bourguignonne for Four
Quick Béarnaise Sauce   *Horseradish Sauce*   *Mustard Sauce*
Rice Pilaf with Mushrooms
Crisp Green Salad with Swiss Dressing
French Bread   Butter
Compote à la Suisse
California Cabernet Sauvignon   Hot Coffee

✿

When you do your shopping, consider the difference in price between meats, and ask your butcher for advice as to tenderness. Some sirloin isn't as tender as others. Shop around for the best value. Usually you can save money by cutting up your own meat. We were very lucky to have found a source for tenderloin tips and trims. Some markets cut tenderloin steaks for restaurants and have a lot of tender scraps left over. These are ideal for fondue, because you end up cutting it in one-inch cubes anyway.

Leftover fondue meat can be frozen, but be sure to wipe the meat dry with paper toweling after it's thawed out or you'll have a lot of splattering and splashing at the table when the moist meat hits the oil.

With this menu we're suggesting a Quick Béarnaise Sauce. If you prefer, make the real Béarnaise Sauce (see index). I like it much better, but the Quick version is easiest for the beginner. You can make the horseradish sauce and mustard sauce ahead and let them stand at room temperature for the flavors to blend until serving time. Freshly grated horseradish is very hot and flavorful and really fun to serve to adventuring gourmets (see the index for reference to how to grate fresh horseradish).

Buy French bread or serve a homemade one (see index). If you choose to serve the rice pilaf with mushrooms, you can slice the mushrooms ahead and have them ready. The last half hour before you plan to serve the meal, start cooking the rice, and combine the rice and mushrooms just before you bring them to the table. This dish holds well, so if you're delayed, or prefer to make this an hour or so ahead, just do it, and keep it hot until you're ready.

The salad greens should be washed well as soon as you bring them home from the market. Dry them, and refrigerate them loosely in a plastic bag. Tear them into bite-size pieces and put them into the bowl hours before you need them, if you wish. Put the dressing on, though, just before you serve it (preferably at the table).

The dessert in this menu is a delightfully refreshing combination of apples, oranges, and kirsch. It should be made ahead so that it can chill. Use pretty dessert dishes for this. To gild the lily you can even serve it with whipped cream.

We suggest a robust Cabernet Sauvignon from California. But, if you prefer, serve a sparkling nonalcoholic Catawba or sparkling apple cider, or just plain coffee.

Beef Fondue Bourguignonne

2 pounds boneless tender beef such as sirloin or tenderloin
about 2 cups salad oil
½ cup clarified butter (see directions below) also is optional
1 teaspoon salt

Pat the meat dry using paper toweling and cut into cubes no larger than one inch. Pile meat into serving bowl. Cover and refrigerate if you do this ahead, otherwise keep it at room temperature for up to one hour before serving time. Fill the beef fondue pot with oil to about half its depth, which will be about two cups. Add the butter (see directions below for clarifying butter). If you prefer, you may use plain butter, omit the butter entirely, or use butter-flavored oil in place of both the salad oil and butter called for in this recipe. Butter is mainly there for the flavor it imparts to the meat as you cook it.

Preheat the oil in the fondue pot on your kitchen range to about 350° to 360° before bringing it to the table. (This step is mainly to save heating time and fuel at the table.) Add salt to the oil in the pot—it will minimize the splattering of the meat if you do have a tiny bit of moisture left on it.

Bring pot with heated oil to the table, set on the special burner, light the flame, and your guests can start cooking by spearing meat cubes one at a time and cooking them in the oil. When meat is cooked to each person's liking, they remove their forks from the oil, spear another piece of meat, put it in to cook, and enjoy the cooked piece with a selection of the sauces you have on the table. This takes time, so be prepared for relaxed conversation and renewed friendships.

To clarify butter, heat it slowly in a pan until melted. Then place in refrigerator to chill until the butterfat is hardened. Pour off the milky liquid that separates out of the butter and remove any foamy covering on the top of the now clarified butter. Clarified butter has a much higher burning point than regular butter and is excellent for many kinds of cooking uses where you need to brown something in a fat.

Horseradish Sauce

1 cup commercial sour cream
¼ cup prepared or freshly grated horseradish
½ teaspoon salt

Blend the sour cream, horseradish, and salt together well. Turn into serving bowl and serve cold. This is *hot*. Makes 1¼ cups.

Quick Béarnaise Sauce

 1 *cup mayonnaise, homemade or high quality commercial*
 ¼ *teaspoon dry mustard*
 6 *peeled, finely chopped green onions, including tops*
 1 *tablespoon tarragon vinegar*
 2 *teaspoons dried tarragon*
 2 *tablespoons softened butter*

Combine all the ingredients together until well blended. Let stand at room temperature for at least ½ hour before serving so that the flavors have time to meld. Makes about 1¼ cups.

Mustard Sauce

 1 *cup commercial sour cream*
 3 *tablespoons prepared hot mustard*
 2 *tablespoons finely minced green onions*
 salt and pepper to taste

Blend the sour cream with the hot mustard. Add the onions, blending in well. Taste and add salt and pepper accordingly. Makes about 1 cup.

Rice Pilaf with Mushrooms

 ½ *pound fresh mushrooms, sliced*
 1 *small onion, sliced*
 4 *tablespoons butter*
 1 *cup uncooked long grain rice*
 2 *cups beef or chicken broth*

In 2-quart saucepan, sauté the mushrooms and onions in the butter over high heat until onion is limp, stirring constantly. Add the rice and stir until rice grains are coated with butter. Pour in the broth, stir to separate the rice grains and cover. Bring to a boil, turn heat down to low and let cook for 15 to 20 minutes or until the rice has absorbed all the liquid. Add salt and pepper at the table. Makes 4 servings.

Crisp Green Salad

1 head Bibb lettuce or Boston lettuce
½ medium-size head romaine or iceberg lettuce
2 to 3 leaves curly endive
4 tablespoons chopped fresh parsley
Swiss Dressing (see below)

Wash all the lettuce, separate leaves, and dry thoroughly. Tear into pieces about 1½ inches in diameter and place in salad bowl. Cover with damp cloth and refrigerate until serving time. Just before serving, drizzle dressing over the lettuce and toss lightly to coat all leaves well. Makes 4 servings.

Swiss Dressing

2 ounces (about ¼ cup) crumbled blue cheese
½ cup mayonnaise
½ cup sour cream
¼ teaspoon salt
⅛ teaspoon pepper
dash garlic powder
2 tablespoons grated Sap Sago cheese (a specialty cheese imported from Switzerland and sold both in cake and grated form)

Blend the blue cheese, mayonnaise, and sour cream. Season with the salt, pepper, and garlic powder. Blend in the Sap Sago cheese and let stand at room temperature until serving time. Sap Sago gives the dressing a wonderful nutlike flavor; add it to cream sauces as well. If you cannot buy it, just omit it from the recipe. Makes about 1¼ cups dressing.

Compote à la Suisse

3 seedless oranges
2 small crisp apples
⅓ cup kirsch, or cherry flavored brandy
whipped cream (optional)

Chill the oranges and apples. Peel the oranges, removing all the white membrane. Divide into sections, catching any juice in a bowl. Remove the membrane from each section. Drop sections of fruit into the bowl with the juice. Core the apples and cut into ½-inch dice. Preferably the apples should not be peeled—however, if they have a disagreeably thick skin, peel them. Blend the diced apples with the orange sections. Add the kirsch and chill for at least an hour before serving. Serve with whipped cream if desired. Makes 4 servings.

Beef Fondue for
a Dozen or Fourteen

❁ We've had some of the best times at beef fondue parties for twelve or twenty-four people. That's why this menu is geared for a dozen or fourteen—so that you can use the same idea. The next menu is for twenty-four and is surprisingly simple to serve.

Last winter fourteen of us—good friends—took off to northern Michigan for a weekend of skiing. We were fortunate enough to be able to rent the quaint old courthouse of Montreal, Wisconsin, because it belongs to a brother of one of the group. The old building is now completely refurbished to accommodate skiers and is set up with two kitchenettes and everything needed.

We still can't decide which was more fun—the skiing, or the fondue combined with the good laughs. Some of us hadn't skied for years, so the day of good exercise at temperatures below zero brought us into the old courthouse in the evening exhausted, exhilarated, *and* hungry.

To stage our fondue dinner we pushed together two dining tables, making one huge table, and put all the chairs around it. We used four fondue pots, one in each corner. There was plenty of room for everything else in the center of the table. As the fondue progressed, the Finn jokes, the Copper Country tales, and the conversation mounted to such a point of hilarity that we ended the weekend sore and stiff from both laughing and skiing.

Our fondue dinner was such a success that we decided to make it an annual event. The menu below is just as we served it, so that if you have a dozen good friends, among them those who can lend a hand in preparation, and fondue pots and forks, you could have just as good a time as we did.

✿

Beef Fondue for a Dozen or Fourteen "Après Ski"
Beef Fondue Bourguignonne for a Dozen or Fourteen
Fresh Grated Horseradish ✿   *Red Hot Sauce*
Onion Sour Cream Sauce
Bulgur Wheat with Mushrooms   Tossed Green Salad ✿
Poppy Seed Dressing ✿   *Caesar Dressing* ✿
Finnish Rye Bread, Minnesota Style ✿   *Butter*
Assorted Cookies ✿   *Mountain Red Burgundy*
Coffee
(✿ indicates things made at home)

✿

Serving the meal was much simpler than the menu looks. To help you out in case you want to do the very same thing we'll outline what we did. The house was equipped with some basics like frying pans and saucepans and silverware.

Equipment brought from home:

4 fondue pots (beef type)	large coffeepot
denatured alcohol for burners	5-ounce disposable clear
14 fondue forks	plastic glasses for the wine
salad bowl	

What we made at home and brought with us:

grated horseradish	prepared salad dressings
cleaned, cut lettuce	bread ready to slice
sliced fresh mushrooms	bar cookies (potluck style)

Other groceries to remember:

fondue meat (6 pounds)
salad oil for cooking (2½
    quarts)
butter (2 pounds)
catsup
mustard
tabasco
mayonnaise

onion soup mix, dry
8-ounce package dairy sour
    cream
bulgur (cracked) wheat
salt and pepper
coffee, cream, and sugar

In getting ready to serve the meal, we divided up the tasks. While one prepared the Bulgur Wheat with Mushrooms and mixed up the sauces, two others cut up the meat. Others set the table, others preheated the fondue pot oil, sliced the bread, got the coffee going, put the salad greens (prepared ahead at home) into the bowl, and the dressings into cups. Someone else arranged the cookies on a tray. Everything was ready simultaneously with no more than 45 minutes' preparation time.

Beef Fondue Bourguignonne for a Dozen or Fourteen

*6 pounds tenderloin or boneless sirloin (we bought 10 pounds
    and used only 6 pounds)*
2½ quarts salad oil for cooking
1 pound butter
4 teaspoons salt
(four fondue pots)

Cut the meat into 1-inch cubes and pile into bowls to bring to the table. Preheat the oil in the pots before bringing to the table and add about ½ cup butter to each pot. If you wish, you may clarify butter at home and add it to the pot instead of the plain butter (see directions on page 19). Put 1 teaspoon salt into each of the four fondue pots to help prevent splattering. Carefully transfer pots onto burners on the table. Light the fire under each pot. Each person spears one piece of meat at a time with his own fondue fork and cooks the meat in the oil until done to his taste.

Red Hot Sauce

½ cup catsup
½ cup prepared mustard
½ cup mayonnaise
3 to 4 drops tabasco sauce
salt and pepper to taste

Blend all ingredients together and let stand at room temperature until serving time. Taste and add salt and pepper if needed plus more tabasco if you want it. Makes about 1½ cups sauce.

Onion Sour Cream Sauce

1 package (about 2 ounces) dry onion soup mix
1 cup (8-ounce carton) dairy sour cream

Blend the onion soup mix and sour cream together. Turn into bowl and serve. Makes about 1 cup.

Creamy Poppy Seed Dressing

This is best done in a blender, but if you don't have one, blend the dressing with an eggbeater until very creamy and smooth.

1 whole fresh egg
⅓ cup white wine vinegar
1 green onion, minced with some of the top
¾ cup sugar
1 teaspoon dry mustard
1 teaspoon salt
2 teaspoons poppy seeds
1 cup salad oil

Put egg, vinegar, onion, sugar, mustard, and salt into blender. Process at high speed until blended together. If you don't have a blender, use a rotary beater. Add the poppy seeds with blender at high speed, and slowly add the oil until mixture is smooth and creamy. Chill. Makes 2 cups.

Tossed Green Salad

1 medium-size head iceberg lettuce
2 medium-size heads leaf lettuce (romaine, Bibb, Boston, etc.)
1 green pepper sliced in thread-thin pieces
1 cucumber, peeled and thinly sliced
3 or 4 red radishes, scrubbed and thinly sliced

Wash the lettuce, breaking leaves apart, dry thoroughly, and tear into pieces about 1½ inches across. Transport lettuce in a plastic bag, the green pepper, cucumber, and radishes in separate bags, all ready to use. Before serving, turn lettuce into a large bowl. Sprinkle with the green pepper, cucumbers, and radishes. Pass the salad dressings at the table. Serves 12 to 14.

Caesar Dressing

This is a dressing that's smooth and creamy; best made in the blender.

3 tablespoons white wine vinegar
2 tablespoons minced green onion
1 teaspoon salt
1 teaspoon dry mustard
½ clove fresh garlic
½ teaspoon coarse black pepper
1 egg
½ cup grated Parmesan cheese
1 cup salad oil

Put vinegar, onion, salt, mustard, garlic, pepper, egg, and Parmesan cheese into blender. Whirl about 2 seconds at high speed, then add the salad oil gradually to make a smooth, creamy dressing. Makes about 2 cups.

Fresh Grated Horseradish

The best way to do this is with a blender. Buy a firm horse-radish root and peel it. Cut it into 1-inch chunks and put about 1 cupful of them at a time in a blender. Add 2 tablespoons vinegar and enough water to the blender to cover the blades. Process until the horseradish is grated. Strain, saving liquid. Put horse-radish into a bowl and cover it while you repeat the process, adding the reserved liquid, to get the remainder of the chunks grated. Add more water if you need it. Refrigerate, *tightly covered* (the fumes can knock you out). This is served just plain —heaped in a bowl. The big dare is to taste the horseradish for the first time. It is guaranteed to clear out clogged sinuses. (Fresh horseradish is delicious on thickly buttered melba toast.)

Finnish Rye Bread, Minnesota Style

If you're not one for making bread, substitute French bread, rolls, or any other personal favorite. I love making bread and like to get the stone-ground rye meal from a Finnish lady on the Iron Range. The natural and organic food stores that sell bulk grain items would probably have stone-ground rye meal, too. If you cannot find it, use rye meal purchased from the supermarket. If you can't find that, substitute whole wheat flour.

> 1 *package active dry or compressed yeast*
> ¼ *cup warm water (lukewarm for compressed yeast)*
> 2 *teaspoons salt*
> 2 *tablespoons sugar*
> 4 *tablespoons salad oil*
> 2 *cups warm water or potato water*
> 2 *cups stone-ground rye meal (or whole wheat flour)*
> 4 to 4½ *cups all-purpose flour*
> 2 to 3 *tablespoons butter, melted, for brushing*

In a large bowl, dissolve yeast in the water. Add the salt, sugar, oil, water, and rye meal. Stir to blend thoroughly. Add the all-purpose flour, stirring until a stiff dough forms. Cover, let stand for 10 minutes. Turn dough out onto a floured board and knead until smooth (about 10 minutes). Butter the mixing bowl well, and put kneaded dough into the bowl; turn it over once and grease the top lightly. Cover, and let rise in a warm place until double in bulk.

Divide dough into two portions. Shape each portion into a smooth round ball. Place in a greased 8-inch round cake pan and press down until dough touches the sides of the pan and is smooth across the top. Repeat with the second half of the dough.

Cover and let rise again until about double in bulk. With a fork, prick loaves all over the top. Put immediately into a 375° oven and bake for about 25 minutes or until loaves sound hollow when tapped with your finger. Remove from oven and from pans, brush with butter, and cool on a rack. Makes 2 loaves.

Bulgur Wheat with Mushrooms

Bulgur wheat comes under many different names in the grocery: bulgur, or bulgour, or the trade name of "ala," or cracked wheat. You can also buy it in health food stores, gourmet shops, specialty shops, and the newly popular natural or organic food stores.

4 cups bulgur wheat
8 cups boiling water
2 teaspoons salt
1 pound fresh mushrooms, sliced
1 large onion, sliced
1 cup butter

Put bulgur wheat into a large (3-quart) heatproof dish. Pour boiling water over, cover, and let stand for 30 minutes. During this time the wheat should absorb all the water. If it hasn't, set over medium heat, stir, and cook about 10 minutes. Add salt. Meanwhile, sauté the mushrooms and onion in the butter until tender (about 5 minutes). Add the wheat, stir to blend, and serve. Makes 12 to 14 servings.

Assorted Cookies for Dessert

We had each lady in the group bring cookies from home to serve as a dessert both for the fondue dinner and for snacking while skiing. The tray looked fantastic with six different kinds of goodies to choose from. Here are our recipes.

Mary's Lemon Bars

These are rich chewy bars that are baked in two steps, first the crust, then the filling. The frosting is lemony tart.

1 cup unsifted flour
½ cup cold butter
¼ cup powdered sugar
2 eggs
3 tablespoons lemon juice
grated rind of one lemon
3 tablespoons flour
1 cup sugar
½ teaspoon baking powder
½ cup grated coconut
powdered sugar frosting (see below)

Measure the flour into a mixing bowl and cut in the butter until the mixture resembles fine crumbs. Blend the sugar into the mixture. Press into an 8- by 8-inch pan and bake in a 350° oven for 20 minutes.

Beat the eggs until light and add the lemon juice and flour, blending in well. Stir in the sugar, baking powder, and coconut. Spread over hot baked crust. Continue baking for another 25 minutes or until top is golden brown, not too dark. Cool. Spread with the frosting. Makes about 18 bars.

Lemon Powdered Sugar Frosting

1 cup sifted powdered sugar
2 tablespoons melted butter
4 teaspoons lemon juice

Blend together the powdered sugar, butter, and lemon juice until mixture is smooth and spreadable. Spread over top of warm bars.

Marge's Sugar Cookies

These are good when handled like refrigerator cookies. All you do is form the dough into rolls about 1½ inches thick, wrap well in waxed paper or plastic wrap, and store in the refrigerator. When you need cookies, slice off what you need and bake the same as directed for rolled out sugar cookies.

1 cup sugar
1 cup butter
2 eggs
pinch salt
3 cups flour
1 teaspoon soda
¼ cup (about) sugar for sprinkling

Cream the sugar with the butter until light and fluffy. Blend in the eggs and salt until dough is smooth. Sift flour with the soda and add to the butter mixture. Chill for about 2 hours or until dough is firm. Roll out very thin and cut out into 2½-inch rounds. Sprinkle with granulated sugar. Bake in 375° oven for about 8 minutes or until light golden in color, not too dark. Makes about 3 dozen.

Quick Crisp Praline Confections

This is one of my favorite "a snap to make" cookies.

20 to 24 graham cracker squares
1 cup butter
1 cup brown sugar
1 cup chopped walnuts

Lay the graham crackers in a 15- by 10-inch jelly roll pan, unbuttered. Combine butter and brown sugar in pan and bring to a boil; boil 2 minutes. Add the chopped walnuts and spoon over the graham crackers. Bake in 350° oven for 10 minutes. Cool and cut into bars. Makes about 48.

Dianne's Butter Pecan Bars

These have a Scandinavian flavor, buttery and nutty.

   4 eggs, beaten until thick
   2 cups brown sugar
   2 cups white sugar
1½ cups butter, melted
2½ cups sifted flour
   2 cups chopped pecans
   1 teaspoon vanilla

Beat the eggs and the brown and white sugar until well blended and frothy. Add the butter, blending in well. Stir in the flour, then the pecans and vanilla. Turn into a 12- by 15-inch jelly roll pan that has been well buttered. Bake in 350° oven for 30 to 40 minutes or until golden. Cut into bars while warm. Makes about 48.

Betty's Date-Filled Cookies

Rolled oats and wheat germ combine to give these cookies a nutritious advantage as well as a nutlike flavor that goes well with the rich date filling.

Cooky Dough
   1 cup butter
1½ cups brown sugar
1½ cups rolled oats
   ½ cup wheat germ
   2 cups flour
   3 teaspoons baking powder
   ½ teaspoon salt
   ½ cup milk

Date Filling
   1 pound dates, pitted and chopped
   ⅔ cup water
   1 teaspoon lemon juice
   ½ cup sugar

Cream the butter and sugar until fluffy. Put the oats into the blender and process until they are ground into a coarse flour, or run through the food grinder twice using a fine blade. Blend with the wheat germ. Sift the flour, measure, sift again with the baking powder and salt. Blend the ground oats and wheat germ into the shortening and sugar mixture. Add the dry ingredients alternately with the milk. Chill dough several hours. Meanwhile, prepare the filling (see below). Roll chilled dough to ⅛-inch thickness. Cut into rounds with a 2-inch biscuit cutter. Put about 2 teaspoons of the filling on half the rounds, cover with the other rounds, and press edges together. Bake on a greased cooky sheet in 350° moderate oven for 12 to 15 minutes. Makes about 4½ dozen cookies.

Date Filling. Combine dates with water, lemon juice, and sugar. Cook, stirring frequently until thickened, about 15 minutes. Cool.

Clarice's Coconut Dream Bars

These are much like Mary's Lemon Bars except for the differently flavored filling on top of the butter pastry.

¼ *cup brown sugar*
1 *cup butter*
2 *cups sifted flour*
4 *eggs*
3 *cups brown sugar, dark or light*
6 *tablespoons flour*
1 *teaspoon vanilla*
1 *cup flake style coconut*
1 *cup chopped pecans or walnuts*

Cream the brown sugar with the butter until light. Blend in the flour until mixture resembles coarse crumbs. Pat into a 9- by 13-inch pan and bake in 350° oven for 15 minutes. Beat the eggs, brown sugar, flour, and vanilla until light. Blend in the coconut and chopped nuts. Spoon mixture over baked layer in pan and continue baking for another 15 to 20 minutes or until filling has set. Makes about 48 bars.

Dianne's Crisp Oatmeal Cookies

There were two Diannes in our group. This is the other Dianne's recipe for good and unusual cookies.

4 cups quick cooking rolled oats
2 cups brown sugar
1 cup salad oil
2 eggs, well beaten
½ teaspoon salt
1 teaspoon almond extract

Blend the rolled oats with the brown sugar, salad oil, and eggs, blending well. Stir in the salt and almond extract. Mix well. Drop by teaspoonfuls onto a lightly greased cooky sheet. If desired, the dough can be made ahead and refrigerated until you're ready to bake cookies. Bake in 325° oven for about 10 minutes or until lightly browned. Remove from pan while hot or they will stick. If desired, you can add nuts, raisins, chopped dates, fruitcake fruit mix, or whatever you like to the cookies for flavor variety. We like them plain. Makes about 4 dozen cookies.

Beef Fondue Bourguignonne for Twenty-Four

1677762

🌞 We had a joyous gathering in our backyard for a dear friend who'd moved away and had come back for a visit. We all wanted to see him and enjoy a meal together, not just any meal, but a memorable occasion on a higher plane than an ordinary potluck supper. Fondue was the answer, for it is, in fact, a friendship dish and seemed to be symbolic of the feeling that tied our whole group together.

We adopted the old maxim "many hands make light work," and did what we could potluck style, including the sharing of fondue pots, card tables and chairs, a few salads, and desserts. It was a lovely, warm Minnesota summer evening and the fondue fires must have chased the mosquitoes away. The occasion was flawless.

Here's the menu:

❀

Beef Fondue Bourguignonne for Twenty-Four
Blender Béarnaise Sauce   Quick Curry Sauce
Mustard Mayonnaise
Garden Green Salad   Spicy Bean Salad
Assorted Hard Rolls   Butter
Summertime Fruit Tray   Ice Cream
California Burgundy   Coffee

❀

Every cook contributed something to the menu, and we shared the cost of the meat and the wine. Sauces, salads, rolls, and butter were set out for the buffet. People helped themselves, then sat down. The meat was at the table, wine and coffee was passed around. The dessert was served buffet style, too.

Beef Fondue Bourguignonne for Twenty-Four

Altogether we used six fondue pots and seated four people to a table. We used plain butter instead of clarified butter this time because we were outdoors and the odors were not a problem; it was simpler to do it that way.

12 pounds tenderloin or boneless sirloin steak
3 quarts salad oil
3 cups butter, divided into ½ cup portions
6 teaspoons salt

Cut the meat into 1-inch cubes and pile into 6 bowls, one for each table. Fill each of six fondue pots about half oil and add ½ cup butter to each one. Add 1 teaspoon salt to each pot to reduce the splattering. Preheat the pots in the kitchen and transfer onto burners just before eating. (Preheat oil to about 350° to 360°.)

Guests then spear pieces of meat and cook them in the hot oil and butter until done to their liking.

Blender Béarnaise Sauce

Triple this recipe to fill up six bowls for the tables or one large bowl for the buffet. You'll have some left over, which you can freeze and use to flavor vegetables, noodles, or pasta. Or you can melt it and pour it over poached eggs, barbecued steak, hamburger patties, or whatever.

2 whole eggs
3 tablespoons white wine vinegar
1 teaspoon dried tarragon
2 tablespoons chopped fresh parsley
2 tablespoons hot water
1 teaspoon salt
2 teaspoons prepared mustard
1½ cups melted butter

Put eggs, vinegar, tarragon, parsley, hot water, salt, and mustard into the blender. Process at high speed a couple of seconds. Then with blender at high speed add the melted butter slowly, processing it about 10 seconds in all. The mixture should be thick and smooth. It will thicken up as it cools off, too.

Makes about 2 cups of sauce.

Quick Curry Sauce

This is a creamy sauce that you can flavor up or down depending on your taste for curry powder. Divide the batch into 6 bowls to bring to the tables, or pile it into one large one for the buffet.

2 tablespoons curry powder
1 carton (12-ounce size) dairy sour cream
¼ cup lemon juice
1 quart mayonnaise (high quality commercial or homemade)
salt and pepper to taste

Blend the curry powder into the sour cream and stir in the lemon juice and mayonnaise until smooth. Taste and correct seasonings. Makes about 6 cups.

Mustard Mayonnaise

1 quart (4 cups) mayonnaise
1 cup prepared mustard
1 cup cider vinegar

Combine the mayonnaise, mustard, and vinegar and blend well. Chill. Divide into six bowls to bring to the tables or turn into one large bowl for the buffet table. Makes about 6 cups.

Spicy Bean Salad

This salad is best made several hours ahead or even the day before so that the flavors can blend together well. Because of the nature of the salad it serves many purposes, and it's a good one to remember whenever you're serving a large group. It could take the place of a relish, vegetable, or starch type dish if you're looking for something to fill these needs with a menu for a large group.

2 cans (16 ounces each) diagonally sliced green beans
2 cans (16 ounces each) diagonally sliced yellow wax beans
2 cans (16 ounces each) kidney beans
2 cans (16 ounces each) garbanzo beans or white beans
¾ cup salad oil
¾ cup white vinegar
¾ cup sugar
2 teaspoons chili powder
1 teaspoon basil
2 cups thinly sliced celery
1 green pepper, minced
1 cup chopped fresh parsley
1 cup chopped green onions
¼ cup capers
1 cup sliced pimiento-stuffed olives
1 can (4 ounces) diced pimientos

Drain all the beans well and put into a large container for marinating. Blend the oil, vinegar, sugar, chili powder, and basil and pour mixture over the beans. Mix well. Cover and marinate for several hours or overnight in the refrigerator. Before serving, mix in the celery, green pepper, parsley, onions, capers, olives, and pimientos. Makes 24 servings.

Garden Green Salad for Twenty-Four

In buying your salad greens, be sure to choose the ones that are fresh and crisp. When you bring them home, wash and dry the lettuce immediately and store in a large plastic bag or covered container in the refrigerator to keep the greens crisp.

2 *heads red leaf lettuce*
2 *large heads Boston lettuce*
2 *heads romaine*
2 *tablespoons tarragon leaves*
1 *cup chopped fresh parsley*
1 *cup olive oil*
freshly ground pepper
3 *teaspoons salt*
⅓ *cup white wine vinegar*
2 *cups crisp herbed croutons, homemade or bought*

Wash the lettuce, separating leaves and drying thoroughly. Tear into bite-sized pieces and put into a big salad bowl. Chill. Just before serving, sprinkle with the tarragon and parsley. Toss. Drizzle a fine stream of oil over it, covering the surface of the lettuce evenly. Sprinkle with freshly ground pepper and then with salt. Toss. Sprinkle evenly with the vinegar and toss well. Last of all sprinkle the croutons over the top and bring to the buffet table. Makes about 24 servings.

Summertime Fruit Tray

This is an attractive way to serve fruit and it can vary according to the fruits that are in season. Choose fruits that will contrast on the tray, and if possible, use berries with sliced whole fruits. If your market is short of fruit you can substitute canned or frozen fruit such as cherries, sliced peaches, mandarin orange sections, pineapple spears, etc. Basically, you should figure on having about 1 cup of fruit per person served. Serve the fruit with a side scoop of ice cream. Choose your prettiest tray for arranging the fruit or a rustic salad bowl that can be quite handsome with the bright fruit piled into it.

melons such as cantaloupe, honeydew, muskmelon, casaba, etc.
cherries, black or red
berries such as strawberries, raspberries, or blueberries
fresh apricots
fresh peaches
fresh grapes such as tokay, seedless, muscat, etc.
fresh or canned orange segments
fresh pineapple
sugar for sprinkling

Peel or wash the fruit and cut into serving-size pieces. Cut melon into pretty slices and arrange on a tray, alternating the fruits according to color and darkness. Use grape clusters to accent the tray. Sprinkle with sugar. Serve with ice cream on the side.

Beefball Fondue for the Family

☀ The fondue pot, once you've invested in it, is too easy-to-use and enjoyable a cooking vessel to save just for special occasions. Here's a fondue that's not of expensive meats, but rather features meatballs. We suggest just one good sauce to make the preparation really simple. You can add catsup, mustard, or other favorite sauces if you wish.

Save your cooking oil and use it over again. Simply strain out all the particles and keep it in a covered jar in the refrigerator. One exception: If you've overheated the oil so that it has exceeded the smoking point, it is not worth saving. Overheating makes the oil break down and produces off flavors immediately. That rancid, bitter taste isn't pleasant.

✿

Beefball Fondue

Potato Puffs   Olive Sauce   Pickle Relish
Catsup   Mustard Olives   Dill Pickles
Peas with Herb Butter
Blueberry Crisp

✿

Even though we're suggesting this fondue for the family, just the idea of using the fondue pot dresses it up enough to make the menu suitable for guests. Grandmas and grandpas, uncles, aunts, cousins, or just good family friends will all enjoy this meal.

To prepare the meal, shape the meatballs and refrigerate them until serving time. Bring frozen, partially thawed 12-ounce package of potato puffs to the table (one commercial variety is called "Tater Tots"). Make the olive sauce just before eating while you're cooking the peas. The dessert can be made at any time earlier in the day.

Beefball Fondue

1 *pound ground round steak, lean, not watery meat (If you buy
    from a reputable meat market they don't water down the
    meat.)*
1 *small onion, minced*
1 *whole egg*
3 *tablespoons flour*
1 *teaspoon salt*
dash *black pepper*
½ *cup milk*
cooking oil, *about 2 to 3 cups depending on the size of your
    fondue pot*
1 *teaspoon salt*

Put meat and onion into a large bowl and mix well. If you have a food chopper, put the mixture through it to make it very smooth and homogeneous. Blend in the egg, flour, salt, pepper, and milk to make a smooth mixture. Shape into balls about 1 inch in diameter. Place in one layer on a large flat pan, like a cooky sheet, serving tray, or cake pan. Chill until serving time. Before serving the fondue, preheat the cooking oil to 360° or 375° on your kitchen stove. Add the salt and set onto the burner on the table. Participants spear the meatballs and cook them individually in the oil until done to their taste.

Have a bowl of thawed potato puffs on the table, too, and everyone can alternate in cooking these with the meatballs. This makes for a leisurely meal. Makes 6 servings.

Olive Sauce

1 large jar (10 ounces) stuffed green olives
1 cup beef broth
½ cup cooking sherry (or substitute broth, if you prefer)
1½ teaspoons minced fresh onion
3 tablespoons each butter and flour

Drain olives; reserve liquid. Slice olives very thinly and set aside. Combine 2 tablespoons of the olive liquid with the beef broth, sherry, and onion in a pan. In a saucepan, melt the butter and stir in the flour to make a smooth paste. Slowly add the liquid mixture, stirring constantly. Cook until thickened. Add reserved sliced olives. Taste and add seasonings, if desired. Makes about 1½ cups sauce.

Peas with Herb Butter

2 packages (about 10 ounces each) frozen baby peas
½ cup boiling water
⅓ cup butter
½ teaspoon dried dill weed, basil, or tarragon
salt and pepper

Cook peas in the water for 8 to 10 minutes; drain. Add the butter, dill or herbs, and salt and pepper to taste. Toss lightly and serve immediately. Makes 6 servings.

Blueberry Crisp

⅔ *cup brown sugar, firmly packed*
½ *cup uncooked rolled oats, quick cooking or regular*
½ *cup all-purpose flour*
¼ *teaspoon salt*
½ *cup butter*
1 *can (about 1 pound) blueberry pie filling*
cream or ice cream for topping

Blend brown sugar, oats, flour, and salt in mixing bowl. Cut in the butter until the mixture is crumbly. Pat half the mixture in a 9-inch-square cake pan. Top with the pie filling. Top with remaining crumbly mixture. Bake in 400° hot oven for 15 minutes or until crumbs are browned. Serve warm with cream or ice cream. Makes about 6 servings.

Stuffed Meatball Fondue

✹ The fondue is great for the family, but you might even serve it as a late evening supper, after a sporting event, the theatre, or whatever. As an appetizer or hors d'oeuvre it rates tops. If you decide to serve stuffed meatballs for a cocktail party, eliminate the remainder of the menu. Arrange the meatballs on a tray and indicate the type of stuffing by using the stuffing ingredient as a garnish.

❀

Stuffed Meatball Fondue
Sour Cream Sauce
Hot Green Beans with Bacon
Cornmeal Spoon Bread
Apple Crisp

❀

45

Make the stuffed meatballs ahead of time, even one or more hours before eating; refrigerate. Mix the sour cream sauce ahead; refrigerate. Prepare the apple crisp and have it ready to bake in preheated oven; then bake it along with the spoon bread 45 minutes before you plan to eat. While the spoon bread and apple crisp are baking you can prepare the green beans with bacon. As usual, preheat the fondue oil before bringing it to the table.

Stuffed Meatballs for Fondue

In buying the ground round for this recipe, be sure to get it from a reputable market where no fat and water are added to the meat. You can tell when ground meat is too watery if the packages are very moist on the bottom where the wrap is sealed. Of course, it is ideal to buy from a butcher who will portion out the meat and wrap it individually for you. Not all of us have this pleasure anymore.

1 pound lean ground round
½ cup cracker crumbs
1 egg
3 tablespoons milk or broth
1 teaspoon seasoned salt
½ teaspoon seasoned pepper (optional)
For filling: stuffed olives; Cheddar cheese cubes, cut to ½ inch;
*   cherry tomatoes; sausage cubes or chunks or small sausages,*
*   pitted ripe olives; pickle cubes, etc.*
2 to 3 cups cooking oil
1 teaspoon salt

Blend the ground meat with the crumbs, egg, milk, salt, and pepper. Using no more than 1 tablespoon of the mixture at a time, form into balls around the filling of your choice. Arrange filled meatballs on a tray in one single layer; cover and refrigerate at least 1 hour before eating. Preheat oil with salt in the fondue pot to about 360° to 375°. Bring meat to table, bring heated oil to table and set on fondue burner. Spear the meatballs on fondue forks and cook in the hot oil until done to individual preference. Serve with the sour cream sauce. Makes 4 servings.

Sour Cream Sauce

This sauce is flavored with dry hot mustard and makes a spicy dip. Substitute other dips and dunks or add others to your menu if you so desire.

1 cup commercial sour cream
2 tablespoons lemon juice or white wine vinegar
1 tablespoon sugar
1 teaspoon seasoned salt
¼ teaspoon seasoned pepper
1 teaspoon dry hot mustard
¼ teaspoon paprika

Whip the cream until smooth and flowing in texture. Blend in the lemon juice, sugar, salt, pepper, mustard, and paprika. Cover and refrigerate until serving time. Makes about 1 cup.

Hot Green Beans with Bacon

When fresh green beans are not available or of good quality you can substitute the fresh frozen variety.

1 pound fresh green beans, cut in 1-inch pieces
2 slices bacon, diced
1 teaspoon salt
dash pepper
⅓ cup salad oil
3 tablespoons catsup
2 tablespoons vinegar
½ cup sliced radishes

Cook the green beans in boiling salted water to cover until tender, about 10 to 15 minutes. (More mature green beans take longer to cook than very fresh, young, tender snap beans which really make more delightful eating.) Drain. Meanwhile, cook the bacon until crisp and drain. Blend the salt, pepper, oil, catsup, and vinegar. Add the radishes to the beans and turn into a preheated serving bowl. Pour the catsup mixture over and toss. Crumble the bacon over the top and serve hot. Makes 4 servings.

Cornmeal Spoon Bread

This is one of my favorites, and when I'm not serving it with a fondue I serve it for Sunday dinner along with an old-fashioned pork roast. Provide hot melted butter to pour over servings, if you really want to gild the lily.

> 2 *cups boiling water*
> 1 *tablespoon butter*
> 1 *cup yellow cornmeal*
> 1½ *teaspoons salt*
> 4 *eggs, separated*
> ½ *cup milk*
> ½ *cup sifted all-purpose flour*
> 2 *tablespoons baking powder*
> 2 *tablespoons sugar*

Boil water in a 2-quart saucepan; add the butter. Sprinkle in the cornmeal; add the salt; stir until smooth, and cook 5 minutes more until thick. Remove from heat and cool. Beat the egg yolks with the milk and stir in. Add the flour sifted with the baking powder and sugar, blending well. Beat egg whites until stiff and fold in. Pour into a greased 2-quart baking dish or soufflé dish. Bake in 375° oven for 40 to 45 minutes. Serve immediately, spooning the bread from the baking dish onto individual serving plates at the table. Be sure to pass melted butter. Makes about 4 servings.

Apple Crisp

> 5 *tart cooking apples*
> 1 *teaspoon lemon juice*
> ½ *cup water*
> ¾ *cup flour*
> 1 *cup sugar*
> 1 *teaspoon cinnamon*
> ¼ *teaspoon nutmeg*
> ½ *cup butter*
> ½ *cup chopped walnuts (optional)*

Peel and slice the apples into a 1-quart casserole. Blend the lemon juice and water and pour over the apples. In a bowl, blend in the flour, sugar, cinnamon, and nutmeg; cut in the butter until the mixture resembles coarse crumbs. Add the nuts if desired. Sprinkle this mixture over the apples. Bake uncovered in 375° oven for 45 minutes. Serve hot. Makes 4 servings.

Poor Man's Lobster Fondue

❄ Norwegian codfish sold under the name of *torsk* has been appearing in the northern midwest markets lately. Scandinavians hail it as being so similar in taste to lobster that it has earned the name "poor man's lobster." The fish is a frozen Iceland codfish fillet of very high quality and makes excellent eating. It can be baked, broiled, or fried, but a new and delightful way to serve it is in fondue style.

❄

Poor Man's Lobster
Drawn Butter   Lemon Wedges
Blender Hollandaise
Golden Toasted Rice   Goddess Salad
Cherry Cheesecake Pie
California Pinot Chardonnay   Coffee or Tea

❄

If you cannot find a fish called *torsk* in your market, then buy Icelandic codfish. If you're fortunate enough, fresh scallops are delightful in place of the *torsk,* but you have to live in the right part of the country to find them today.

To prepare the meal, partially thaw the fish before cutting it up (scallops need not be cut). The fish should be thawed and very well dried (pat dry with paper toweling) before making the fondue or you will have excessive splattering. Except for the dessert, this menu can be prepared in the last half hour before serving.

Poor Man's Lobster Fondue

½ pound torsk, *Norwegian or Icelandic codfish, or fresh scallops per person served*
2 to 3 cups cooking oil
1 teaspoon salt
lemon wedges

Partially thaw the meat before cutting. With a heavy sharp knife, cut the meat into 1-inch cubes. Dry well with paper toweling and allow to thaw completely before making the fondue. Place fish cubes in a single layer on a serving tray lined with paper toweling; cover and refrigerate until serving time.

Preheat the cooking oil to 360° or 375°; add the salt and bring to the table; place on fondue burner. Guests spear pieces of the fish and cook about 45 seconds to 1 minute or until done to their own taste. Have drawn butter in individual soufflé cups, and dip each piece of cooked fish into the butter while eating. Serve lemon wedges in a bowl.

Drawn Butter

Melt ¼ cup butter per person in a heavy pan over low heat. When butter is bubbly but not at all browned, divide into individual soufflé cups or custard cups for serving.

Golden Toasted Rice

1½ *cups uncooked long grain rice*
 3 *tablespoons butter*
 3 *cups beef broth*
 6 *green onions, chopped*

Put rice into a saucepan or frying pan with the butter and sauté rice until butter is golden and rice becomes opaque. This will take about 5 minutes; stir constantly. Add the beef broth and onions and bring to a boil. Stir to separate rice grains. Cover, turn heat down to low, and let simmer for 25 to 30 minutes. Rice should have absorbed all the liquid by this time and be fluffy and dry. Serve hot. Makes 6 servings.

Goddess Salad

¼ *head crisp iceberg lettuce*
¼ *head romaine*
about 18 medium-size radishes
 1 *can (2 ounces) anchovy fillets, minced*
 2 *medium-size tomatoes, peeled and diced*
 1 *tablespoon chopped fresh parsley*
¼ *teaspoon oregano*
freshly ground pepper

The Dressing:

½ *cup olive oil*
 2 *tablespoons white wine*
     vinegar
½ *teaspoon salt*
¼ *teaspoon coarsely ground*
     pepper
 2 *tablespoons mixed salad herbs*
     (blend of marjoram, rosemary,
     tarragon, savory, chives, cher-
     vil, parsley)
 2 *bunches green onions*

Tear lettuce into bite-size pieces and put into salad bowl. Add whole cleaned radishes, anchovies, tomatoes, parsley, oregano, and pepper. Toss.

For the dressing, shake the oil, vinegar, salt, pepper, and herbs together in a jar. Pour over salad greens. Poke green onions (trimmed, derooted, washed, and dried) into the salad with the green tops standing out. Serves about 6.

Blender Hollandaise Sauce

3 egg yolks
1 tablespoon lemon juice
1 tablespoon hot water
½ teaspoon salt
dash cayenne
1 teaspoon prepared mustard
1 cup melted butter

Combine egg yolks, lemon juice, hot water, salt, cayenne, and mustard in the blender. Blend at low speed about 5 seconds. Pour melted butter into blender going at high speed, adding butter gradually. Makes 2 cups.

Cherry Cheesecake Pie

This is a happy combination of pie and cheesecake. It's easier to make than a cheesecake and has the serving characteristics of a pie.

1 package (8 ounces) cream cheese, at room temperature
¾ cup sifted powdered sugar
1 teaspoon vanilla
1 cup whipping cream, whipped stiff
1 baked 9- or 10-inch pie shell
1 can (about 1 pound) cherry pie filling

Put cheese into mixing bowl and blend in the sugar and vanilla. Fold in the whipped cream. Pour into the baked pie shell. Top with the cherry pie filling and chill about 3 hours before serving. Makes 6 servings.

Mixed Grill Seafood Fondue

There are so many frozen seafoods on the market that are all ready to heat and eat that it would be a shame not to take advantage of them for a fondue. One of the tastiest ways to serve these handy ready-breaded shrimp, crab, scallops, and little fish puffs is to thaw them almost completely, and cook them crisp in the fondue pot.

You might consider keeping these items on hand in your freezer for drop-in company, or for a quick-to-fix snack. This is a delightful answer to the problem of appetizers or hors d'oeuvres when you have a party, too. Just be sure that you keep unused portions very well wrapped in the freezer to prevent frost buildup or drying out. I like to have a variety of frozen fish on hand so that I can pick and choose a mixed group for each fondue meal. It's easy to provide for more or fewer people this way, too.

❀

Mixed Grill Seafood Fondue
Lemon Wedges   *Tartar Sauce*
Citrus Salad   *Honey Dressing*
Green Rice Casserole
Refrigerator Rolls   *Butter*
Pink Confetti Sherbet

❀

You can always be prepared to serve a mixed grill seafood fondue. Let your variety be dependent on what's available *and* good in quality. You can buy the breaded broken shrimp if the pieces aren't too small. Look for crab puffs, breaded shrimp, breaded scallops, fish sticks, and breaded fish fillets. To serve them, you can place a selection of fish on individual plates or arrange them attractively on a large serving tray. Thaw them completely before you bring them to the table or the cooking time will be just too long. Also, if the oil gets very hot and the fish pieces are still frozen, you're likely to come out with very darkly browned fish on the outside that's cold on the inside. Cut larger fish pieces into 1-inch cubes, particularly the fish sticks and breaded fish fillets.

Make or buy your tartar sauce (see the recipe below). You can use the lemon wedges as a garnish on the tray on which you serve the fish. The tangy citrus salad is a nice contrast to the fish flavor.

We give a recipe for refrigerator rolls, but you can buy them if you're not in the mood for baking. This dough will keep in the refrigerator for 3 or 4 days, so it is a handy one to keep in mind if you prefer to bake your own. You can bake the Green Rice Casserole right along with the rolls during the last minutes before dinner. The dessert is a frozen fruit concoction that's really refreshing and good. Plan to make it several hours ahead or the night before so it will have plenty of time to freeze.

Mixed Grill Seafood Fondue

*4 to 6 ounces frozen prebreaded seafood (shrimp, scallops, crab
    puffs, etc.) per person
2 to 3 cups cooking oil
1 teaspoon salt*

Remove seafood from freezer 1½ to 2 hours before you plan
to serve it. Arrange on serving tray or on plates. Preheat cooking
oil to 360° or 375°; add the salt (to prevent splattering), bring
to the table, and place on lighted burner.

Each person spears seafood of his choice and cooks it until
golden (45 seconds to 2 minutes). Do not refreeze the fish if you
have leftovers, so plan your amounts carefully according to the
predicted appetites of your diners. If need be, you can always
take more from the freezer and take a little longer cooking the
pieces. This is an especially good plan because toward the end
of a fondue you're not as impatient to eat and the oil is hotter,
therefore you'll be able to thaw and cook the pieces sufficiently.

Tartar Sauce

*1 cup high quality mayonnaise, homemade or commercial
4 tablespoons sweet pickle relish
1 tablespoon minced parsley
1 tablespoon vinegar*

Combine all ingredients together and chill until serving. Leftover sauce can be covered and refrigerated for use another time.
Makes about 1¼ cups.

Honey Dressing

*¼ cup honey
½ cup mayonnaise
½ teaspoon celery seed
¼ teaspoon paprika
 1 tablespoon lemon juice*

Combine honey, mayonnaise, celery seed, paprika, and lemon

juice; mix well. Chill for about 1 hour to blend flavors. Makes about 1 cup dressing.

Citrus Salad

1 large head iceberg lettuce
3 large navel oranges
2 ripe pears
1 sweet Spanish onion (if you cannot get it, see suggestion below)

Core, rinse, and drain the lettuce. Refrigerate. At serving time, separate outer leaves and line serving bowl or platter with them. Shred remaining lettuce and pile in the center. Peel and slice the orange crosswise. Core pear and slice into thin wedges. Slice and separate onion into rings. Arrange fruit and onion rings over lettuce. Serve with honey dressing (see below). Makes 4 to 6 servings.

If you cannot buy sweet Spanish onions, buy a large white onion. Peel it and slice it very thinly. Put into a colander and set it in a large bowl. Cover with boiling hot water. Let stand 1 minute. Remove onion by lifting colander. Immediately rinse with very cold water. This process will release much of the tear jerk from the onion.

Green Rice Casserole

3 cups cooked rice
1 cup chopped parsley
¾ cup shredded Swiss cheese
⅓ cup minced onion
1 teaspoon salt
3 beaten eggs
1½ cups milk
1½ teaspoons Worcestershire sauce

Blend rice, parsley, cheese, and onion together and turn into a buttered 1 or 1½ quart casserole. Mix salt, eggs, milk, and Worcestershire sauce and stir into rice. Bake in a 350° oven for 30 minutes. Makes about 6 servings.

Refrigerator Rolls

This is a yeast batter that you can stir up and keep in the refrigerator. It will keep 3 to 4 days, and to bake you simply remove what you need, returning the remaining dough to the refrigerator. It's great for cinnamon rolls, too (which are good for breakfast, and so we included that recipe just in case . . .).

1 *package active dry yeast*
2 *cups lukewarm water*
½ *cup shortening*
½ *cup sugar*
½ *cup cold mashed potatoes*
½ *cup dry powdered milk*
2 *eggs*
6 *cups flour*
½ *teaspoon salt*
1 *teaspoon baking powder*
¼ *teaspoon soda*

Dissolve the yeast in ¼ cup of the water and let stand for five minutes. With the electric mixer, beat the shortening, sugar, mashed potatoes, powdered milk, eggs, and ½ cup of the water together until blended. Add the remainder of the water and mix until blended. Stir in the yeast mixture and 3 cups of the flour until mixture is like thick cream. Cover and let stand until bubbly. Add the remaining 3 cups of flour along with the salt, baking powder, and soda. Turn out onto a lightly floured board and knead only about 12 times just to make the dough hold together and to blend the flour in well. Turn into a greased bowl, cover with waxed paper and a damp cloth. Or turn into a plastic container that has an airtight lid and keep refrigerated and use as needed.

To use, remove a portion of the dough, shape into buns, and place on a greased pan. Let rise 4 to 5 hours (less in warm weather), and bake for 15 minutes in a 400° oven. Makes about 4 dozen rolls.

For cinnamon rolls, roll dough out flat on a lightly floured board. Spread with softened butter and sprinkle with a mixture of cinnamon and sugar. Roll up as for a jelly roll and slice about 1 inch thick. Place cut side down in pan. Let rise 4 to 5 hours. Bake 15 minutes at 400°. Frost with powdered sugar mixed with a little hot coffee to make a thin glaze.

Pink Confetti Sherbet

　2 *medium-size ripe bananas, mashed*
　1 *cup orange juice*
　¼ *cup fresh lemon juice*
1½ *cups sugar*
　1 *cup milk*
　1 *cup water*
　¼ *cup chopped red maraschino cherries*
　3 *tablespoons juice drained from maraschino cherries*

Mix bananas with orange and lemon juices. Add sugar, milk, water, cherries, and cherry juice, mixing well. Pour into a refrigerator tray or loaf pan of about 1½ quart capacity. Freeze until firm. Remove from freezer, break into chunks, and put into large bowl. Beat smooth with rotary beater. Return to freezer pan, cover, and freeze until firm. Makes about 1½ quarts.

Ham Fondue for a Casual Easter Dinner

A ham is a ham, but when it's cut into chunks it makes great fondue-ing. Sure breaks the monotony of cooking one thing the same way all the time. When you're buying a ham for your Easter Ham Fondue, be sure to select a good one. The flavor's better if the ham has been cured slowly and smoked naturally. Canned hams are just not suitable for a ham fondue—they're much too stringy and soggy. The boneless variety is easy to cut into one-inch chunks, but don't let that be your only criterion. If you adore pea or bean soup made with a ham bone, you've got one once you've cut away the meat. But when you're buying a ham with the bone in, especially if it's only half a ham, check to be sure you're not buying the end with all the bone. It may look nice on the cut surface, but when you get it home you could discover that the nice little bone that was showing grows bigger and bigger as you cut through the meat. Best of all buy a *shankless* ham. That's the one with the "aitch" bone removed. It's *always* good to ask your meat man about the ham, or even have him cut one for you. Find out what brand it is. If it's good, later you'll ask for the same kind again—or vice versa.

This menu will serve eight to ten people, so plan to have two fondue pots going. Borrow one if need be.

✿

Ham Fondue

Fresh Grated Horseradish   Sweet-Sour Sauce
Broccoli Casserole   Fruit Salad Supreme   Cream Dressing
Cornmeal Muffins   Butter
Lemon Crunch Dessert

✿

Ham fondue for an Easter dinner is great if you're short on preparation time for your meal. Again, you can make the fruit salad ahead and refrigerate it (the flavor's better that way), and you can make the dessert ahead. Cornmeal muffins are very good with this, and made from scratch at the last minute, they add a real homey touch to the whole menu. Bake the Broccoli Casserole along with the muffins. You can assemble it at any time ahead. It bakes for thirty minutes.

Ham Fondue

¼ to ½ pound lean boneless precooked ham per person
1 quart salad oil

Cut ham into cubes about 1 inch square. Wipe as dry as possible with paper toweling and put ham cubes into serving bowls. Divide oil between the two fondue pots. Preheat them to 360° or 375° before bringing to the table. Place on lighted fondue burners. Add a dash of salt to minimize splattering. Each person spears a ham cube, and cooks it just long enough to heat through in the hot oil. Eat with the sauces provided. You may have a favorite sauce you'd like to add or serve in place of those suggested. See index for instructions on how to grate fresh horseradish.

Sweet-Sour Sauce

1 small can (8-ounce size) crushed pineapple
¼ cup vinegar
¼ cup well-packed brown sugar
few grains pepper
½ teaspoon paprika
2 chicken bouillon cubes, crushed
2 teaspoons prepared mustard
2 tablespoons cornstarch
½ cup water

Combine crushed pineapple (juice and all), vinegar, sugar, pepper, paprika, bouillon cubes, and mustard in pan and bring to a boil. Stir until bouillon cubes are dissolved. Blend cornstarch with water and stir into the sauce. Cook, stirring until clear and thick. Watch carefully because this sauce will burn easily. Makes about 2 cups. Store leftover sauce in the refrigerator; it keeps well.

Broccoli Casserole

2 packages (10 to 12 ounces each) frozen whole broccoli
1 can (10 ounces) cream of celery soup
¼ cup milk
dash Worcestershire sauce
¼ cup soft bread crumbs blended with 2 tablespoons melted butter

Cook broccoli as directed on the package, but undercook it, reducing the cooking time by 5 minutes. Put broccoli into a buttered 1-quart casserole. Mix soup, milk, and Worcestershire sauce. Pour mixture over the broccoli. The casserole may be covered and refrigerated for later baking at this point. Just before baking sprinkle with the buttered bread crumbs. Bake in a hot oven (400°) for 15 minutes or until bubbly. Makes 8 to 10 servings.

Fruit Salad Supreme

1 can (1 pound 5 ounces) apricot pie filling, chilled
2 large bananas, sliced
2 large apples, cored and diced

1 *small cantaloupe, cut in 1-inch cubes*
2 *large fresh pears, cored and diced*
¼ *cup finely chopped nuts*
¼ *cup minced celery*

Blend all ingredients together lightly. Turn into a serving dish. Pass the cream dressing (see below) around at the table to spoon over helpings of the salad. Makes 8 to 10 servings.

Cream Dressing

½ *cup mayonnaise*
½ *cup whipping cream, whipped*
1 *tablespoon lemon juice*
¼ *teaspoon celery seed*

Fold mayonnaise into the whipped cream. Blend in the lemon juice and celery seed. Turn in to serving bowl. Makes about 1¼ cups dressing.

Cornmeal Muffins

If you butter the muffin pans liberally and put them into the oven to heat while the batter is being mixed they will come out with crusty brown sides.

1 *cup all-purpose flour*
1 *cup yellow cornmeal*
2 *tablespoons sugar*
2 *teaspoons baking powder*
¼ *teaspoon soda*
1 *egg, beaten*
1 *cup buttermilk*
2 *tablespoons melted butter or margarine*

Sift flour, cornmeal, sugar, baking powder, and soda into mixing bowl. Blend egg, buttermilk, and butter and stir into dry ingredients only enough barely to mix; the batter will be lumpy, but don't try to smooth it. Drop into heated muffin pans and bake in a hot oven (400°) for 20 minutes or until golden. Makes 12.

Lemon Crunch Dessert

This is a dessert that is to be frozen, so plan to make it the day before or early in the morning of the day you plan to serve it.

¼ *cup butter*
⅓ *cup well-packed brown sugar*
1½ *cups wheat flakes*
⅓ *cup chopped walnuts*
 3 *egg whites*
½ *cup white sugar*
 3 *egg yolks*
 1 *cup whipping cream*
juice and rind of 1 lemon

Melt butter in a pan and stir in the brown sugar until it is completely dissolved. Blend in the wheat flakes and nuts. Spread in a 9-inch-square pan and let cool. Then crumble it. Reserve half crumbled mixture for topping.

Beat the egg whites until frothy and gradually add the sugar, beating until stiff. Next, using the unwashed beaters, in another bowl, beat the egg yolks until light and fluffy. In still another bowl, using the same beaters, whip the cream until stiff and then beat in the lemon juice and rind. Now, fold all three mixtures together (the whites, yolks, and cream). Put half the crumbled mixture into the pan, top with the lemon cream mixture, and sprinkle the reserved crumbled mixture over the top. Cover with plastic wrap and freeze until hard. Cut into squares to serve. Makes about 10 servings.

An Appetizer Fondue Party

❉ Fondues make easy-on-the-hostess appetizers for a party, especially if there is a large number of people. Fondues come off with such a flair that your guests think you've slaved hard to prepare when actually they're about the simplest thing to serve.

You can check over all the fondues in this book and most of them are perfectly adaptable for serving as an appetizer at a party. In this menu we're suggesting three different fondues that work very well. The amounts given are sufficient for fifty people. You can easily divide the amounts in two for a group half the size. When we did the testing, I found that it wasn't always easy to find punch recipes that weren't terribly sweet, but that packed a little punch, without becoming astronomical in cost. We just had to improvise a few of them, too. One punch bowl is all you really need, but if you're ambitious and need two, by all means use two. We're giving several recipes for you to choose from.

*

Beef and Lamb Appetizer Fondue
Bagna Cauda
Shrimp and Cheese Fondue
Punch

*

To prepare for the party, do your shopping the day before. The day of the party, make the Bagna Cauda dip first, cover, and set aside. Then cut up the beef and lamb and prepare the sauces for them. Assemble the ingredients for the shrimp and cheese fondue, but put it together last of all. Prepare the vegetables for the Bagna Cauda, cover, and keep them cold until ready to serve.

Decide on the punch the day before the party. If you aren't sure of your guests' tastes, it might be well to have one that is nonalcoholic along with a larger amount of the other.

Just before the party, set the three fondues on the tables. It's best to locate them in different parts of a home or room if you want the guests to circulate. Outdoors, it's easy to separate the punch and the food, but just be sure that the tables you use are sturdy and well balanced so that hot fondues will not be spilled accidentally.

It's smart to have an extra supply of the fondue ingredients on hand just in case one of the fondues is really popular and the demand for it continues. Otherwise, you can resign yourself to the fact that when one runs out, guests will have to concentrate on the others.

Beef and Lamb Appetizer Fondue

3 *pounds boneless sirloin or tenderloin*
3 *pounds boneless leg of lamb*
1 *large package frozen potato puffs*
5 *cups cooking oil*

A choice of three sauce recipes follows.

Trim beef and remove fat and gristle. Cut into 1-inch cubes. Trim fat from lamb and cut into 1-inch cubes. Cover and refrigerate until party time. Put potato puffs into a bowl and thaw completely before serving. Fill the sauce dishes. Just before serving, heat oil in fondue pot to about 375°. Transfer to lighted burner on serving table. Be sure that the table and the fondue burner are steady. Provide bamboo skewers for people to use to cook cubes of meat and potato puffs. Guests cook one piece at a time, dip it into a sauce, and eat, using a slice of bread to catch drips. Makes about 50 appetizer servings.

Bagna Cauda

½ *cup olive oil*
¼ *pound butter*
4 *cloves garlic, mashed*
6 *anchovy fillets, finely minced*
1 *head celery, cut into pieces 1½ inches long*
1 *head fennel, cut into pieces 1½ inches long*
2 *green peppers, cut into strips ½ inch by 1½ inches long*
1 *large cooked artichoke, ready for plucking*
¼ *pound large raw mushrooms, quartered*
1 *pint cherry tomatoes*
1 *cucumber, peeled, quartered, and cut into 2-inch sticks*
1 *head cauliflower, cut into flowerets, each one halved*
1 *head Belgian endive, cleaned and leaves separated*
1 *head romaine, cleaned, leaves separated*
6 *zucchini about 5 inches long, scrubbed, trimmed, sliced diagonally*
1 *loaf thinly sliced snack rye bread, slices halved*

Combine the olive oil, butter, garlic, and anchovies in a fondue pot. Heat until butter is melted, stir to blend all ingredients well. Set pot over low flame, just hot enough to keep the mixture warm. The butter must not burn.

Choose about 5 of the vegetables suggested above and arrange them on a serving tray or in salad bowls. Guests pick a piece of vegetable, dip it into the sauce, and use a slice of rye bread to catch drips. Makes 50 appetizer servings.

Shrimp and Cheese Fondue

2 *pounds uncooked shrimp, shelled and deveined*
boiling salted water
¼ *cup butter*
¼ *cup flour*
1 *teaspoon salt*
1 *cup light cream or half-and-half*
1½ *cups white wine*
1 *tablespoon sherry*
½ *pound white brick cheese, diced into* ½ -*inch pieces*
½ *teaspoon paprika*
1 *large crusty loaf French bread cut into 1-inch cubes*

Cook shrimp in the boiling water until just pink; drain and set aside. Melt the butter in a fondue dish over medium heat; stir in 2 tablespoons of the flour and the salt; cook until it bubbles, stirring constantly. Gradually add the cream, cooking until slightly thickened and smooth. Blend in the white wine and sherry. Dust the diced cheese with the remaining 2 tablespoons flour and add slowly to the boiling mixture, stirring until the cheese is melted. Add the paprika. Stir in the shrimp. Bring to the table and place on burner set at a very low heat. Provide the French bread cubes for dipping along with skewers, forks, or toothpicks. Makes 50 appetizer servings.

Old-Fashioned Hollandaise

If you would like to make a quicker version of hollandaise sauce, check the index of this book for blender hollandaise.

¼ *pound butter*
4 *egg yolks*
2 *teaspoons lemon juice*
pinch white pepper
pinch salt

Divide the butter into three portions. In top of a double boiler, or in a heatproof bowl set over hot water, put the 4 egg yolks and 1 part of the butter. Stir the mixture rapidly and constantly with a whisk over hot, but not boiling, water until butter is melted. Add the second piece of butter, whipping constantly. As the mixture thickens and butter melts, add the third part, whipping so as to scrape the bottom and sides of the bowl well. Do not allow the water to boil.

When the butter is melted and mixed well, remove the saucepan or bowl from the water and continue beating 2 minutes longer. Whip in the lemon juice, pepper, and salt. Should the mixture curdle and separate, immediately beat in 1 or 2 tablespoons boiling water to rebind the emulsion. Makes about 1 cup.

Sparkling Wine Punch

1 large can (12 ounces) frozen concentrated orange juice
½ gallon California Rhine wine, chilled
4 cups California brandy, chilled
¼ cup fresh lemon juice
2 quarts sparkling water, chilled

Reconstitute the orange juice as directed on the can. Blend orange juice, wine, brandy, and lemon juice in punch bowl. Add 2 quarts cracked ice and let stand for about 1 hour. Just before serving, add more ice and the sparkling water. Makes about 50 4-ounce servings.

Rush 'n Punch

1 large can (12 ounces) frozen concentrated orange juice, thawed
2 quarts sparkling water, chilled
1 bottle (4/5 quart) vodka, chilled
2 quarts crushed ice

Mix the punch immediately before serving. Blend orange juice, sparkling water, and vodka in punch bowl. Add the ice. Stir well. Makes about 25 4-ounce servings.

Almost-Authentic Indian Curry Sauce

This sauce is great with the lamb. Dip into this sauce and then into a dish of coconut for an especially interesting flavor combination.

```
 ½  cup finely chopped onion
 3  tablespoons butter
 1 ·cup diced green apples
 2  tablespoons flour
 2  teaspoons curry powder
 ½  teaspoon salt
dash nutmeg
dash cayenne
 1  small clove garlic
 1  small bay leaf
 3  tablespoons chopped fresh parsley
 1  medium onion, thinly sliced
1½  cups rich chicken stock
```

Cook the chopped onion in the butter until onion is golden, about 5 minutes over medium heat. Add the apple and simmer for another 5 minutes. Remove from heat and sprinkle with the flour, curry powder, salt, nutmeg, and cayenne. Blend well.

In a saucepan combine the garlic, bay leaf, parsley, sliced onion, and chicken stock. Simmer until stock is reduced by half. Strain it. Stir the hot stock gradually into the apple mixture. Bring the sauce to a boil and cook, stirring constantly until it thickens and bubbles. Place over hot water and simmer another 5 to 6 minutes, stirring occasionally. Taste, correct seasoning, and pour into a serving bowl. Be sure to reheat the sauce before serving if you make it ahead. Makes about 1½ cups.

Simple Sparkling Punch

```
 2  cans (46 ounces each) pineapple-grapefruit juice drink, chilled
 ½  cup fresh lemon or lime juice
 1  quart chilled ginger ale
ice in a block
```

Combine the pineapple-grapefruit juice drink and the lemon or lime juice in a punch bowl. Add a block of ice. Just before serving, add the ginger ale. Makes about 25 4- to 5-ounce servings.

Horseradish-Applesauce

This is especially good with beef. Any left over, you might try it with pork or ham.

1 cup applesauce
½ cup freshly grated horseradish (see index)

Combine the applesauce and horseradish together well. Chill. You can make the sauce hotter by adding more horseradish. Makes 1½ cups.

Butter Caper Sauce

½ cup butter
1 tablespoon lemon juice
¼ cup capers, drained
salt

Melt the butter over a low flame and skim off the foam. Add the lemon juice and capers and add salt to taste. Makes about ¾ cup sauce.

Remoulade Sauce

2 cups mayonnaise
½ cup finely chopped sour pickles
2 tablespoons finely chopped capers
1 tablespoon prepared mustard
1 tablespoon chopped parsley
1 teaspoon tarragon

Combine the mayonnaise with the pickles and capers. Add the mustard, parsley, and tarragon. Let stand about ½ hour for flavors to blend before serving. Makes about 2½ cups sauce.

Thanksgiving Turkey Fondue

❄ For the nonconformist who wants to conform just a little, we present a turkey fondue for Thanksgiving that's a snap to serve. Cook the turkey breast meat in the fondue pot. All the trimmings still remind you of the traditional Thanksgiving meal. You may add or subtract from the menu as you desire, but we're including everything, beginning with the appetizer punch and ending with a traditional dessert. The amazing thing is that most of the dishes can be made ahead, so there's no worryng about carving the beast, and the actual meal can be rather effortless so that you, the hostess-cook, can really enjoy the meal and your guests.

You have the choice of buying the whole turkey, dissecting it, removing breast meat and dark meat for the fondue, saving the remainder for stock or soup, or, you can buy just the breast meat, dice it, and you're ready. If you wish, you may buy a boned turkey roll, cut it into one-inch pieces, dark meat and all, and the preparation is done.

If you are a small family (like two or four), you could substitute chicken for the turkey and make adjustments in the menu to suit your group.

❁

Pumpkin Soup   Croutons
Turkey Fondue
Orange Relish   Whole Cranberry Sauce
Almond Stuffing   Giblet Gravy
Assorted Mixed Pickles   Green and Black Olives
Romaine Salad with Assorted Cheeses
Cornbread   Butter
Mincemeat Brandy Pie with Ice Cream

❁

Because the Orange Relish needs to stand a couple of days to blend its flavors, you'll make that first. You can make the Whole Cranberry Sauce at the same time and have that all done. The day before the meal you can make the Pumpkin Soup, assemble the dry ingredients for the stuffing, and make the Mincemeat Brandy Pie. The day of the meal, assemble and bake the stuffing, make the gravy, salad, and cornbread, and cut up the meat. You buy the pickles and olives.

Pumpkin Soup

2 tablespoons butter	1 tablespoon butter
4 chopped green onions	2 tablespoons flour
1 small white onion, sliced	¾ cup hot light cream
4 cups raw pumpkin, peeled and diced, or 2 cans (16 ounces each) cooked pumpkin	salt and pepper
	1 tablespoon butter
	toasted croutons for topping (serve in bowl at table)
4 cups chicken broth	1 cup heavy cream, whipped, for topping (optional)
½ teaspoon salt	

Melt the butter in a 2-quart saucepan; add the green onions and sliced white onion. Cook 5 minutes, stirring, over medium heat until onion is cooked but not browned. Add the pumpkin (raw or canned), add the chicken broth and salt. Simmer until pumpkin is soft, or about 15 minutes. Blend the butter with the flour and whip it into the hot soup. Cook until soup is thickened. Taste and add salt and pepper if needed. (Soup can be refrigerated at this point.) Heat just to the boiling point and add the cream and 1 tablespoon butter. Serve as an appetizer in the living room, if desired, passing the bowls of croutons and cream, or serve at the table as a first course. Makes about 10 first course servings.

Turkey Fondue

½ pound raw boned turkey or turkey breast meat per person
2 cups cooking oil per fondue pot
¼ cup butter per fondue pot

Cut turkey into 1-inch cubes and place in a bowl that's been lined with paper toweling to absorb any liquid that might drain from the meat. This occurs especially with frozen turkey. Preheat oil in the fondue pot in the kitchen to about 360° or 375°. Bring to the table and add the butter to the pot. Place fondue pot over burner. Add a dash salt to minimize splattering. Each guest spears cubes of turkey with his fondue fork and cooks it in the oil for a minute or two until the meat is done to taste.

Orange Relish

1 pound fresh cranberries
1½ cups granulated white sugar
3 large seedless oranges
2 tablespoons curaçao, Cointreau, or Triple Sec

Wash, drain, and dry the cranberries. Put through the coarse blade of the food chopper once. Put in a bowl and add the sugar.

Peel the oranges using a potato peeler to remove the "zest" (the orange-colored part of the peel) of the orange only. Peel off the white skin. Put the flesh of the orange and the zest through the food chopper, cutting the orange into small pieces first. This is a juicy job, so be sure to put the bowl beneath the grinder to catch the drips. A better way is to do your grinding in the blender, processing both the cranberries and the orange just until coarse but not fine in texture. Blend the orange and the curaçao very well with the cranberries. Put into a jar or crock and cover. Refrigerate several hours before serving. Better yet, a day or two. Makes about 1½ quarts. This relish keeps well.

Whole Cranberry Sauce

1 cup sugar
1 cup water
½ pound (2 cups) whole fresh cranberries

Put sugar and water into a saucepan and cook until the sugar is dissolved. Wash the cranberries and drain well. Add to the sugar-water mixture and cook for 5 minutes or until cranberries stop popping. Don't stir. Cool in the pan. Makes about 3 cups sauce.

Giblet Gravy

While we're on the subject of raw turkey, chicken, giblets, etc., a word of warning. Be sure to wash your cutting board in hot soapy water when you've finished cutting up raw poultry, and *before* you cut anything else on it. Salmonella bacteria are very commonly found in raw poultry. They will contaminate your cutting board, and in turn you can contaminate other food items you might cut on it. Salmonella bacteria will cause a common type of food poisoning if allowed to grow, spreading in your stuffing mixture, or even on cooked meat. They are killed off by cooking, but it is possible to recontaminate cooked meats, stuffings, etc., by the use of an unwashed cutting board and utensils after the foods are cooked.

turkey giblets and neck
  2 quarts water
  1 teaspoon salt
few celery leaves
½ cup butter
½ cup all-purpose flour
salt and pepper to taste

Put giblets and neck from the turkey into the water. Add the salt and celery leaves and simmer for 2 hours. Remove giblets and dice them very fine. In another pan, melt the butter and add the flour. Slowly add the hot broth from cooking the giblets (there should be about 6 cups). Cook until thickened, stirring until blended. Taste and add salt and pepper. Pass gravy at the table to pour over the stuffing and to dip cooked cubes of turkey. Makes about 6 cups gravy.

Almond Stuffing

  1 cup minced onion
  1 cup melted butter
  1 cup thinly sliced celery
  1 teaspoon salt
  2 teaspoons poultry seasoning (commercially available blend
      of thyme, marjoram, savory, and sage)
  5 cups toasted stale bread crumbs or unseasoned prepared
      stuffing croutons
1½ cups toasted slivered almonds
About 2 cups turkey or chicken broth (if you are boning a turkey
      for the fondue you may wish to make a broth using the
      bones, giblets, etc., otherwise use canned prepared chicken
      broth)

Cook the onion in the butter until golden. Blend in the celery, seasonings, bread crumbs, and almonds. Add enough broth to make the stuffing hold together. Turn into a 2-quart casserole and bake in 350° oven for about 1 hour or until golden.

Romaine Salad

1 large head crisp romaine
1 head Boston lettuce
4 tablespoons olive oil
2 tablespoons red wine vinegar
2 teaspoons mixed salad herbs
salt and pepper to taste
crumbled feta cheese, shredded Cheddar cheese, diced Swiss
cheese to pass at table for topping individual salads

Wash the romaine and Boston lettuce leaves separately, removing all grains of sand; dry well. Tear into bite-size pieces and put into a salad bowl that's been rubbed with a cut clove of garlic. Sprinkle the olive oil over it, then the vinegar, and then the salad herbs. Toss well. Add salt and pepper to taste. Pass bowls of cheese at the table. Makes 8 to 10 servings.

Cornbread

1¼ cups sifted all-purpose flour
¼ cup yellow cornmeal
1 tablespoon baking powder
1 tablespoon sugar
½ teaspoon salt
3 tablespoons shortening
1 egg
⅓ cup milk

Sift flour, cornmeal, baking powder, sugar, and salt into a bowl. Cut in the shortening until the mixture is like fine bread crumbs. Beat egg and combine with the milk; add all at once to the flour mixture and stir lightly with a fork. Place on floured board and knead very lightly and quickly to make a smooth ball of dough. Roll out into a square about ¾ inch thick; cut into 1¼ inch squares. Place on a greased baking sheet and bake in 450° oven for 12 minutes. Makes 8 to 10 servings. Serve immediately.

Mincemeat Brandy Pie

pastry for a 2-crust pie
3½ cups prepared mincemeat
¼ cup brandy

Roll out pastry to fit a 9-inch pie pan; flute the edge. Roll out the remainder to make cutouts appropriate for Thanksgiving such as pilgrim hat, turkey silhouette, etc. Moisten the mincemeat with the brandy and pour into the pastry-lined pan. Put cutouts on top. Bake in 450° oven for 10 minutes. Reduce heat to 350° and continue baking for 15 minutes or until pastry is nicely browned. Makes 8 servings. Serve with scoops of ice cream, if desired.

A Fondue and Wine Sampling Party

☯ For a unique party plan we suggest that you serve nothing but fondue. Mixing and matching the fondues with a selection of wines can test the memories and palates of your guests.

For this menu you'll need five fondue pots: one for a cheese type fondue (heavy pottery pot); three of the type used for beef fondue; and one dessert type with a candle for a burner. Don't be afraid to borrow fondue pots from your friends. But if you do, *please* return them cleaned and polished.

If you plan this menu among cooperative friends, you may get fondue pots and go potluck on the wines, making suggestions for a red, white, apéritif, or cordial type wine for them to bring. You might even have them hide the labels so that the wines are a mystery. Besides adding to the fun, this is a good way to share the cost of a party.

To stage the party, plan to have each type of fondue separated from the others, and the appropriate wines around each fondue pot. You might direct people toward starting with apéritif type wines and the fondue appetizer tarts, then on to the cheese fondue with white wines, the beef fondue with claret, the Bagna Cauda with Chianti or Burgundy, and the chocolate fondue with fruits and the cordial wines. Although this menu will serve many people, there's guesswork involved and it would be best to have spare ingredients in the kitchen just in case. This menu should serve 20 to 24 people easily with the amounts given here.

✿

Empañadas in Fondue
Dry Sherry
Cheese Fondue Neufchâteloise   Gewürtztraminer or Riesling
Fondue Bourguignonne   California Cabernet Sauvignon
Bagna Cauda   Italian Chianti
Chocolate Fondue
Chenin Blanc (light, sweet white wine), port, or muscatel

✿

Do these things in advance: (1) Shape the empañadas and arrange on a serving tray; chill until party time. Remember to get bamboo skewers or fondue forks for cooking them. (2) Cut up the cheese and mix it ready with the flour and seasonings, in amounts enough for one batch at a time (keep one or two as spares in the refrigerator—they'll keep well if you don't use them for your party). (3) Cut up the meat for the beef fondue, and about 1 hour before, make the Béarnaise Sauce (see p. 37); keep it at room temperature. (4) Clean and cut the vegetables, arrange on a serving tray. Put the ingredients for the Bagna Cauda dip into the pot you'll be using; heat it up at party time. (5) Arrange fruits on a tray for the chocolate fondue. Immediately before serving, melt the chocolate into the warm cream. It's so convenient you don't have to worry about it until the last minute, but it's also so simple to reheat that you can make the chocolate dip ahead and then reheat it at serving time. Guests will probably wander back and forth from fondue to fondue for quite awhile before they're ready for the chocolate fondue.

Plan the locations of the fondues well ahead of party time so that you'll be able to separate the wines, provide for trays of vegetables or whatever without the last-minute rush. If desired, this menu can be served almost without dishes (provide lots of napkins).

Empañadas in Fondue

> *1 cup flour*
> *1 small (3-ounce) package cream cheese*
> *¼ cup butter*
> *1 to 2 tablespoons ice water*
> > *1 tube (2 ounces) anchovy paste, or a 2-ounce can of deviled ham*
> > *3 cups cooking oil*

Sift flour, measure, sift again into a mixing bowl. Cut in the cream cheese and butter until the mixture resembles coarse crumbs. Sprinkle water over to make a stiff pastry dough. Chill. Roll out to about ⅛ inch thickness and cut into 2-inch rounds. Put about ¼ teaspoon anchovy paste or deviled ham in the center of each round. Fold over and seal well by pressing edges with a fork. Place on a serving tray and chill until party time. Heat oil in the fondue pot to 375° and set on lighted burner at party time. Guests will spear each empañada with a fondue fork or wooden skewer and cook their own pastries in the hot oil until it's golden. This will take about 2 minutes. Watch the oil so it doesn't overheat; follow directions that come with the fondue pot to control the flame carefully. Makes about 70 empañadas.

Cheese Fondue Neufchâteloise for a Crowd

Don't try to double the recipe for this one because it just won't work as well. Have additional shredded or diced cheese and extra wine on hand to make a fresh batch in case you need it. This takes just a few minutes to prepare.

> 1 *clove garlic, peeled*
> 5 *cups dry white wine such as Rhine, Riesling, or Traminer*
> 2½ *pounds (about 5 cups) shredded or diced Switzerland Swiss*
> *cheese, or domestic Swiss cheese that has been aged 90*
> *days or more. Or, use half aged domestic Swiss cheese and*
> *half domestic mild white cheddar or "natural brick" cheese*
> 5 *tablespoons flour*
> *freshly ground pepper*
> 1 *teaspoon salt*
> *two dashes nutmeg*
> ½ *cup Kirschwasser (Swiss cherry brandy)*
> 2 *large loaves crusty French bread, cut in 1-inch chunks with*
> *some crust left on each piece*

Rub a 2-quart earthenware, pottery, or enameled cast-iron casserole with the garlic (cut in half). Add the wine and heat until bubbles rise to the top, but the mixture isn't yet boiling. Blend the cheese with the flour until the cheese pieces are well coated. Add about ⅓ of the cheese pieces at a time to the simmering wine. Stir, using a wooden spoon, making figure eights in the bottom of the pan. This is to be certain that the center of the bottom gets adequate agitation so it doesn't stick or burn. Continue adding cheese until it is all used up. Add the seasonings and Kirschwasser. Bring to the fondue burner at party time and set on a low flame, just high enough to keep the fondue pleasantly hot, but not so that it will burn. Bread chunks should be put in a basket nearby so that the guests can spear them and dunk into the cheese mixture. Each guest should stir the fondue as he or she dunks into it. If the fondue becomes too thick, add a little warmed wine. If you have trouble with the fondue separating, add a bit more Kirschwasser mixed with some flour; stir it in to thicken. Once the cheese has separated badly (and this can happen if you allow it to get too hot), there's really nothing you can do to return it to the consistency it ought to be. Even separated, though, the fondue has a wonderful flavor and makes for quite pleasant chewing.

The crust that forms on the bottom of the casserole is a special treat, so let your guests fight over it.

This recipe makes about 20 appetizer servings. Served alone, this would be enough for 10 persons.

Fondue Bourguignonne for an Appetizer Party

See the basic directions for Fondue Bourguignonne on page 18. For a party of 20 to 24 people, you'll need to provide about 5 pounds of meat. Make a double batch of the Béarnaise Sauce (see page 37). Have ready a loaf of French bread sliced very thin for guests to catch drips on if you don't provide plates for eating. Beef Fondue Bourguignonne is always a favorite among beef-eaters, so have a couple of pounds of extra beef on hand to replenish the supply if needed.

Bagna Cauda

See directions for Bagna Cauda on page 67. This makes an excellent appetizer fondue because the flavors of anchovy, garlic, butter, and vegetables go together so well. The activity of dipping vegetables into the seasoned butter is ideal for this type of party. Bagna Cauda is especially popular with women. Have a selection of 5 or 6 different kinds of vegetables arranged on a tray artistically. Be sure to think of color when you plan and buy your supplies.

Chocolate Fondue

This is a relative newcomer to the fondue scene, but a real natural. In making Chocolate Fondue you should be especially careful not to overheat the chocolate or it will separate into a very hard substance. Many domestic chocolates are difficult to melt. If possible, buy imported chocolate, and never let the cream come to a boil. To guard against overheating the cream use a double boiler.

1 cup light cream such as half-and-half (half heavy cream, half milk)
20 ounces milk chocolate
3 tablespoons rum, cognac, Kirschwasser, Kahlúa, or any favorite fruit-flavored liqueur

Tray of fruits for dipping:
fresh strawberries
1-inch banana cubes
fresh peach wedges
fresh apple wedges

fresh pear wedges
1-inch cubes of cantaloupe
seedless grapes

Put cream into the top of a double boiler and heat over boiling water for 5 minutes. Break the chocolate into the cream and stir until melted. Once the chocolate is melted, turn heat down and add the desired flavoring. To serve, pour into a chocolate fondue pot, or set over a candle warmer. Have the fruits attractively arranged on a tray or in bowls around the hot chocolate fondue. Have a supply of toothpicks, bamboo skewers, or fondue forks handy for guests to spear fruit and dunk into the sauce. Makes enough for 20 to 24 people.

❋

Lamb Fondue with Curry Condiments

❋ This is a delightful idea for lamb curry fanciers. Cook lamb cubes in hot oil in your beef fondue pot. Then, along with the lamb, serve rice and all the condiments that might go along with curry, plus a really good curry sauce. A Zinfandel would be the ideal red wine to serve to make the meal special.

❋

Lamb Fondue
Coconut Sambal   Pineapple Chutney
Radish Pickle Relish
Chopped Peanuts   Cucumber Yogurt Sauce
Sliced Bananas
Indian Rice   Vegetables Kerie
Orange Ice Cream

❋

To prepare this dinner, have your meat man bone a leg of lamb. You may even be able to get him to cut it into 1-inch cubes for you. This is a job that requires a very sharp knife. In preparation, it's best to get the radish pickle relish done first because it needs to stand for 2 hours before eating to blend the flavors. The Coconut Sambal and the Pineapple Chutney can be made at any time in advance and should be served at room temperature. Cook the rice just before serving. If you prefer, you can substitute Fluffy Rice (see the index) for the Indian Rice. The vegetables are in a curry-flavored sauce and should be prepared just before serving and served hot. Make the Orange Ice Cream the day before so that it will have time to freeze, or substitute a lime sherbet, if you wish.

Lamb Fondue

½ pound boneless cubed leg of lamb per person
2 to 3 cups cooking oil for the fondue pot

Have your meat man bone, trim, and cut up the meat for you. The lamb should be cut into 1-inch cubes. Preheat the cooking oil in the fondue pot in the kitchen to about 375° before bringing it to the table to place on the lighted burner. Spear pieces of meat with fondue forks and cook as for beef fondue, a piece at a time until it is done to your liking. Spoon the relishes and sambals and sauces onto your dish and dip cooked pieces of meat into them before eating. A delightful combination is to dip the cooked meat into the Cucumber Yogurt Sauce, then into chopped peanuts.

Coconut Sambal

1 cup grated coconut
2 teaspoons dry hot red chili pepper (more or less according to taste)
1 medium-size onion, minced
1 tablespoon sugar
3 cloves garlic, chopped
salt to taste

Combine all ingredients in a small frying pan. Cook for 20 minutes over medium heat until browned and dry. Makes about 1 cup.

Cucumber Yogurt Sauce

1 *medium-size cucumber*
2 *green onions*
½ *cup unflavored yogurt*
¼ *teaspoon salt*

Peel the cucumber and cut into chunks; put into the blender. Cut green onions into ½-inch pieces and put into the blender. Add the yogurt and process until the sauce is coarse, not smooth— just a few seconds. Add the salt. Makes about 2 cups of sauce.

Indian Rice

2 *cups long grain rice*
4 *cups water*
3 *tablespoons butter*
1 *teaspoon salt*
1 *medium onion, chopped*
1 *cup dried currants or light raisins*
½ *cup chopped walnuts*
3 *tablespoons salad oil*
½ *teaspoon curry powder*
1 *teaspoon salad oil*
saffron the size of a grain of rice
1 *tablespoon hot water*

Put the rice and water into a large kettle. Add the butter and salt. Bring to a boil and simmer until the rice has absorbed all the water, about 20 minutes. In a frying pan, sauté the onion, currants, and nuts in the oil until the onions are transparent but not browned (about 7 minutes). Stir in the curry powder mixed with the 1 teaspoon oil. Pour this mixture over the rice and blend in well. Dissolve the saffron in the hot water and mix into the rice. Serve immediately. Makes 6 to 8 servings.

Pineapple Chutney

1 tablespoon salad oil
1 small onion, sliced
2 hot (fresh) red chili peppers, diagonally sliced (available through markets that specialize in unusual or foreign produce)
Or if you cannot get the fresh, use dried red chili pepper to taste
1 can (14 ounces) pineapple chunks, drained
1 teaspoon ground cinnamon
3 tablespoons sugar

Heat oil in a pan and add the onions. Cook for 1 minute and add the red pepper, cooking 1 to 2 minutes more over medium heat until onions are limp. Add remaining ingredients and simmer 10 minutes. Makes about 1½ cups.

Radish Pickle Relish

2 bunches radishes
1 tablespoon salt
½ cup vinegar
3 tablespoons sugar
¼ cup water

Scrub radishes well, cut off root end and stem ends. Slice them thin and put into a dish. Sprinkle with the salt and let stand for 20 minutes; drain. Heat vinegar and add the sugar, add the water and boil 2 minutes. Remove from heat and cool. Add the radishes. Let stand at least 2 hours before serving. Makes about 2 cups.

Vegetables Kerie

1 tablespoon salad oil
½ medium-size onion, minced
3 cloves garlic, minced or mashed
1 tablespoon curry powder

 1 *tablespoon ground coriander*
 1 *teaspoon ground caraway seed (crush with mortar and pestle)*
 2 *bay leaves*
½ *cup water*
 1 *large green pepper, sliced ¼ inch*
 1 *cup fresh cabbage, cut in 1-inch squares*
 2 *cups green beans, cut in 1-inch pieces*
 1 *cup cucumbers, cubed to 1-inch size*
salt to taste
 2 *cups chicken or beef broth*

Heat the oil in a large pan and add the onion and garlic; cook for 2 minutes over high heat. Add the curry powder, coriander, caraway seed, bay leaves, water, green pepper, cabbage, green beans, and cucumber. Bring to a boil, reduce heat to low and cook 10 minutes. Add the salt and broth and cook until vegetables are tender. Makes 6 to 8 servings.

Orange Ice Cream

 2 *cups whipping cream*
 2 *cups milk*
1½ *cups sugar*
 2 *cups freshly squeezed orange juice*
½ *cup freshly squeezed lemon juice*
 2 *tablespoons grated orange rind*
 2 *tablespoons grated lemon rind*

Whip the cream. Stir the milk with the sugar until dissolved. Blend with the cream. Pour into refrigerator trays and freeze until mushy (about 1 hour). Blend in the orange and lemon juices and the rinds from the orange and lemon. Freeze, stirring two or three times until the ice cream is solid. Makes about 2 quarts.

Lamb Fondue for the Family

☀ This menu is considerably simpler to do and less expensive than the preceding one. It's based on ground lamb that's available on the meat counter of most meat markets. They're often in the form of patties. They're simple to reshape into little balls for fondueing.

✿

Ground Lamb Fondue
Curried Rice with Onions   Zucchini Sauce
Bananas and Coconut   Mango Chutney (commercial)
Peaches in Plum Sauce

✿

For this menu you need to find a market that sells ground lamb, or you might talk to your meat man, maybe he can order it for you if it isn't a regular item with him. The price is comparable to ground beef or hamburger. If it is very coarsely ground you may want to put it through the fine blades of a food chopper, or ask your butcher to do it for you. The rice and onions are a family favorite of ours that is quick to stir up. The dessert can be made ahead and chilled, and the two curry accompaniments are easy to put together at the last minute.

Ground Lamb Fondue

⅔ to ¾ pound ground lamb per adult, ¼ to ½ pound per child
2 to 3 cups cooking oil
¼ cup butter for the fondue pot (optional)

Shape the ground lamb into balls about 1 inch in diameter or smaller. Put on a tray for serving. Preheat oil in the fondue pot in the kitchen to about 375°, then bring it to the table and place on a lighted fondue burner. Each person will spear the meatballs and cook them in oil. You'll notice that the meatballs must be very well compacted if the lamb is coarsely ground. We'd recommend grinding coarse-ground lamb once or twice (see suggestion above), to help the meatballs to hold together.

Curried Rice with Onions

4 tablespoons butter
1 cup coarsely chopped onions
1 cup long grain rice
2 cups chicken broth
2 teaspoons curry powder

Melt the butter in a heavy cooking pot or casserole and add the onions. Stir and cook until onions are soft (about 5 minutes). Add the rice and chicken broth. Turn heat down to low. Cover and cook for 20 minutes. Season with the curry powder before serving. Makes about 4 servings.

Zucchini Sauce

1 small zucchini, peeled
2 green onions
½ cup yogurt (unflavored)
¼ teaspoon salt

Cut zucchini into 1-inch chunks. Put into the blender with the green onions, yogurt, and salt. Blend at low speed until sauce is coarsely granular (not smooth). Refrigerate until serving time or serve immediately. Makes about 1 cup.

Bananas and Coconut

2 medium bananas, not overripe, but slightly green
2 tablespoons lemon juice
½ cup flaked coconut

Peel the bananas and slice them in ¼-inch slices into a bowl. Sprinkle with the lemon juice and top with the coconut. Pass at the table to eat as a condiment with the ground lamb fondue. Makes 4 servings.

Peaches in Plum Sauce

¾ cup sugar
3 tablespoons water
8 red plums
6 or 7 peaches

Combine the sugar and water in a saucepan and boil gently for 5 minutes. Pour this syrup over the plums and cook at low heat for 10 minutes or until the skins burst. Strain the juice and purée the plum pulp. (Press through a sieve, or pit and peel and whirl in blender.) Peel and slice the peaches and put them into a serving bowl. Pour the plum juice mixed with the plum pulp over the peaches and chill thoroughly before serving. Makes 4 servings.

Japanese Tempura, Fondue Style

❁ Tempura is the classic Japanese fritter that's becoming more and more popular as an appetizer. With the advent of the fondue pot, it's quite achievable as a main course for a meal. Though slightly different from some of the fondues we've been talking about, the action is much the same. If you apply the each-one-cook-for-himself principle of fondue the tempura adapts itself to the long leisurely eating characteristic of the fondue style.

The traditional "tempura pot" or cooker is shaped like a basin with two handles and a grate on one side to drain the fritter-like pieces when they're cooked. (See the illustration.) To do it fondue style, in a fondue pot, you'd simply do any draining you desire right on your dinner plate. Or, you might provide a paper napkin folded into a small square as a pad for draining pieces of the tempura.

Setting the table for tempura is fun if you've got the traditional Japanese things to use. You might serve sake. It should be served warm, and the little sake cups are really fun to use. Rustic Japanese dishes or pottery add atmosphere, although plain white dishes are equally authentic looking. Three-cornered baskets are available that are used for tempura. Stuff a paper napkin into a basket, draining the tempura fritters before you eat them. Chopsticks are the order of the day, too. Each place setting should have a teacup (Oriental style), a bowl for the tempura sauce about the size of a soup cup, and a couple of little dishes for condiments (which you can do without if you put the condiments on a dinner plate, Occidental style). A fork is handy for those who can't master the chopsticks. Use either fondue forks or long wooden bamboo skewers for cooking. It's nice to have a supply of hot damp cloths for wiping your fingers, too.

❀

Hot Clear Broth
Japanese Tempura, Fondue Style
Steamed Rice (optional)
Tempura Sauce   Grated Fresh Ginger   Mock Daikon
Warm Sake   Hot Tea
Cherry-Peach Cup

❀

To prepare this meal, you'll need a sharp knife to slice a selection of meat and fish and arrange them on a tray. You'll cut up vegetables, too, and arrange them on another tray. These are then all ready to bring to the table. The soup is a simple concoction which you can make and keep hot until you're ready to eat. Put the Tempura Sauce into individual bowls at each place setting. Pass bowls of grated fresh ginger and Mock Daikon (real daikon is a large white root vegetable that's available only in special Oriental markets, not generally available throughout the United States). If you choose to serve hot rice, you may either serve individual bowls of it, or pass around a bowl of rice.

Have the tea and sake on a warming tray along with the supply of rolled-up damp towels.

Plan on serving a maximum of six people per tempura or fondue pot. Four is really ideal. You may choose to have eight people and then use two fondue pots or tempura cookers (they're not expensive when you can find them, and you can put them right onto your fondue burner).

Japanese Tempura, Fondue Style

Plan on ½ pound per person of your choice of:
   raw shrimp, shelled, tail on, deveined, washed, drained
   lobster, raw, shelled, cut into ¼-inch slices
   scallops, fresh, raw, washed, and drained
   bass, whitefish, or lake trout, sliced in ½-inch by 2-inch pieces
   lean beef, sirloin or tenderloin cut into ½- by 2-inch pieces

Plan on ½ to ¾ pound per person of your choice of:
   fresh asparagus, tough ends removed, cut into 2-inch pieces
   celery, cleaned, washed, dried, cut into 2-inch pieces
   carrots, peeled, and cut into ¼-inch pieces diagonally
   zucchini, washed, sliced into ¼-inch crosswise pieces
   yellow summer squash, sliced into ¼-inch crosswise pieces
   Chinese pea pods, cleaned and dried
   green pepper, seeded, washed, and dried, cut into ½-inch strips
   cauliflower, cleaned and cut into flowerets
   mushrooms, cleaned and dried (should be fresh and small)
   green onion, stems removed, cut into 2-inch strips
   eggplant, washed, dried, cut into slices ¼-inch thick

Tempura batter (see below)
2 to 3 cups cooking oil, preferably peanut oil, per pot

Prepare all the fish, meat, and vegetables as indicated in the listing above. Arrange them on trays; cover and refrigerate until serving time. Have the tempura batter in convenient bowls at the table (2 guests may share a batter bowl). Each guest will dip his choice of fish, meat or vegetable into the batter, drain to get rid of runny drips, then plunge it into the cooking oil. It will be cooked when the fritter is lightly golden in color.

Preheat the oil to about 375° in the kitchen before bringing it to the table and place on burner.

Tempura Batter

    4 eggs, lightly beaten
    2 cups minus 2 tablespoons cold water
1½ cups unsifted flour
    ½ teaspoon salt

Beat the eggs and water until frothy. Stir in the flour and salt. Keep cold by setting the bowl in another bowl filled with crushed ice. This keeps the tempura batter at a good consistency for dipping. You can get along without the bowls of ice if you prefer. This makes enough for 8 persons.

Hot Clear Broth

6 cups chicken broth
2 tablespoons Japanese-style soy sauce
chopped green onion to garnish

Heat broth to boiling; add the soy sauce, garnish servings of the broth with the green onion. Makes 8 small servings.

Steamed Rice

2 cups long grain rice
4 cups water
2 teaspoons salt
2 teaspoons butter

Measure rice, don't wash it. Heat water, salt, and butter in a saucepan to boiling. Sprinkle in the rice slowly. Cover tightly and cook over high heat until the steam starts to come out from under the lid. Then turn the heat to very low and let the rice steam for 20 minutes. Don't peek. Makes 8 servings.

Tempura Sauce

4 cups fish stock or water
1 cup Japanese soy sauce
1 cup sake (Japanese rice wine) or sherry
dash salt

Combine the water, soy sauce, sake, and salt and bring to a boil. This makes 6 cupfuls, enough for eight people. Dip the cooked tempura fritter into this sauce to season it lightly.

Grated Fresh Ginger

Buy fresh ginger in specialty food stores or supermarket produce departments that specialize in unusual items. Many supermarket produce managers are able to order fresh ginger for you if you allow plenty of time. I don't bother to peel the ginger root, but simply grate it on the medium blades of the vegetable grater. If you wish, you can grate it in the blender by following the directions that come with the blender. Serve the grated ginger straight, with nothing added, piled in a bowl. You spoon a bit onto your plate and use it to dip the cooked tempura in before eating. For eight people about 1 cupful of grated ginger is sufficient. You may store leftover ginger in the freezer. (Grated ginger enhances flavors when added to teriyaki marinades, Oriental meat dishes, etc.)

Mock Daikon

By all means, if you *can* get the fresh daikon, use it.

⅔ cup grated red radishes
⅓ cup grated fresh turnip

Blend the radishes and turnip together. Serve in a bowl to pass around at the table. Makes 1 cup. (Note: don't store extra Mock Daikon, even well covered; it does terrible things to the aroma of your refrigerator—it took me several days to figure out what it was that was flavoring the butter.)

Cherry Peach Cup

3 cups pitted sweet cherries, preferably fresh (or use frozen)
3 cups diced fresh peaches (or frozen, well drained)
½ cup Japanese or Chinese cherry cordial
sugar for sprinkling (optional)

Combine the cherries and the peaches and blend the cherry cordial in well. Chill for several hours. Have sugar available at the table for guests to add if desired. Makes 8 servings.

The Original Swiss Feast—
Classic Swiss Cheese Fondue or
Fondue Neufchâteloise

(Dedicated to pretty ladies and handsome partners)

☀ This is the original, the *beginning* of the whole fondue thing. Fondue Neufchâteloise is my everlasting favorite because it is the original fondue and has that *authentic* flavor. The key to making cheese fondue, Swiss style, is getting the right cheese. The very finest is imported Emmentaler from Switzerland which produces a classic flavor. To lighten the flavor the Swiss sometimes use up to 50 percent Swiss Gruyère, which is a milder cheese and is easier to melt. Domestic Swiss cheese just doesn't have the perfect flavor of a good Emmentaler. (The flavor *isn't* bad. It's just *different*.) The only domestic Swiss that works well is one that has been aged. The package often says "aged over 90 days." Usually this is to explain why the higher price. Don't gamble your white wine on an unaged cheese. You may end up with something that has the consistency of bread dough.

On to the menu. This is—ah, the original favorite of our portly Swiss fellow who loved the pretty Swiss girls as much as the fondue. And, if you wish, carry out the classic rule about the dropped bread and the kissing. Or make up your own. Just be sure to enliven the atmosphere with warm colors on the table, soft candlelight, and music.

❀

Fondue Neufchâteloise
Crisp French Bread Cubes
Green Salad with Oil and Vinegar (optional)
Dry White Riesling or Rhine Wine   Kirschwasser
Hot Tea   Fruit Salad (optional)

❀

Swiss Cheese Fondue is traditionally made and served in a stub-handled dish called a *caquelon*. You must use a pot that is not metal, such as earthenware, crockery, or enameled cast iron, or the fondue will quickly burn. You should supply each guest with two forks, one for eating and one for dipping.

This much you can do ahead: have the cheese shredded or finely diced, coated with flour, ready for use. Have the wine already measured and in the fondue pot ready for heating. Start heating the wine when you're sure everybody has arrived and the table is set and ready for the entrance of the fondue pot. Have the salad ready for tossing with oil and vinegar. Cut up the French bread into cubes and pile them in a basket. It is traditional to serve the Kirschwasser about halfway through the meal. Instruct your guests to swirl their bread chunks in a figure eight motion so that the fondue will be stirred constantly, preventing burning. There will be a golden crust on the bottom of the pot. This is a highly prized and tasty ending to the fondue.

Swiss Fondue Neufchâteloise

1 pound Switzerland Emmentaler cheese, or half Emmentaler and half Swiss Gruyère
3 tablespoons all-purpose flour

1 *clove garlic, cut*
2 *cups dry white wine*
3 *tablespoons Kirschwasser or brandy*
nutmeg, few grains
salt and pepper to taste
2 *loaves crisp crusted French bread, cubed to bite size, each*
   with some crust on it

Shred the cheese coarsely or cut it into ¼-inch dice. Add flour to the cheese and mix until cheese pieces are all evenly and lightly coated with the flour.

Rub the fondue pot with the cut edge of the garlic. Pour in the white wine and heat until bubbles rise from the bottom. Add about one third of the floured cheese, stirring briskly with a wooden spoon. *Don't allow mixture to boil.* When the cheese is melted, add the remaining portions, one third at a time. Stir briskly. Stir in the Kirschwasser or brandy. Add a sprinkle of nutmeg and the salt and pepper. Transfer fondue pot to lighted burner on the table. Be sure to adjust the flame so that it doesn't get too hot and burn the fondue. Guests will spear a piece of bread and dunk it into the sauce, swirling a figure eight each time. Makes 4 servings.

Green Salad with Oil and Vinegar

1 *head lettuce, Bibb, Boston, red, or garden*
½ *teaspoon tarragon leaves*
olive oil
vinegar
salt and pepper

Wash lettuce well, pat dry and chill thoroughly. Tear into bite-size pieces and put into a salad bowl. Sprinkle tarragon leaves over it. Just before serving, drizzle oil over leaves in a thin stream, making a large circle around the edge and then an X through the center. Sprinkle all over with vinegar. Taste, and add more vinegar, if necessary. Sprinkle with salt and freshly ground pepper. Toss well. Taste. Correct seasonings. Makes 4 servings.

Fruit Salad with Sour Cream

2 cups green grapes, pitted and halved
4 tablespoons brown sugar
½ cup dairy sour cream

Divide the grapes among four dessert dishes. Sprinkle each with 1 tablespoon brown sugar. Divide the sour cream among the four dishes and smooth the top so that all grapes are covered. Chill until serving time. Makes 4 servings.

Fondue à l'Américain

It isn't difficult to make an excellent cheese fondue using American-made cheeses. The preparation procedure is the same as for the authentic Swiss, but the selection of cheese used in this recipe is more easily available, less expensive, therefore less of a shock to the average cook.

When you go cheese shopping, you'll discover that there are several kinds and varieties that are white, not yellow. Most of them melt very easily and well. You can get some delightfully flavored fondues by using such regional cheeses as Casino, Lemke Brick, White Natural Brick, and even one called Svea Ost. They make excellent fondues. They don't taste like Swiss Neufchâteloise, but they have flavors of their own that are very good.

Your total menu can be identical to the Classic Fondue Neufchâteloise, or you can vary it a bit. Here's another suggestion:

❀

Hot Mixed Vegetable Juice
American Cheese Fondue
Mandarin Salad   Italian Dressing
American Trifle

❀

This menu is one that will please most members of the family. It's a practical idea when entertaining houseguests and you want to serve meals that are a little different. Get the dessert done early because it needs to stand for 2 hours. Vegetable juice (commonly sold as V-8 juice) is great served hot in punch cups in the living room. Pass a tray of crackers, too, if you wish. The Mandarin Salad adds a fruity touch to the menu, as most cheeses complement fruit flavors very nicely.

If you're worried about using wine in the fondue, here are two important points: (1) All the alcohol evaporates at about 140° so it's safe for children or people who dislike wines—so use the wine without fear. Or, if you prefer, (2) Substitute apple cider for the wine.

Hot Vegetable Juice

1 quart mixed vegetable juice
6 to 7 dashes tabasco
3 tablespoons fresh lemon juice

Heat the vegetable juice, tabasco, and lemon juice to the simmering point. Serve hot. If desired, you can top each serving with a small pat of butter. Makes about 6 servings.

American Cheese Fondue

½ pound (8 ounces) mild white Cheddar or brick cheese or other soft white cheese that melts smoothly to a non-stringy consistency (mozzarella won't work)
½ pound (8 ounces) domestic Baby Swiss cheese that is labeled "aged over 90 days"
3 tablespoons all-purpose flour

1 clove fresh garlic
2 cups dry white wine, Rhine, Riesling, or Chablis
1 tablespoon lemon juice
salt and pepper to taste
1 large loaf crusty French bread, cut in 1-inch cubes, each
*   with some crust on it*

Shred cheese coarsely or cut into ½-inch dice. Mix with the flour until all pieces of cheese are well coated. Rub the fondue pot with the cut edge of the clove of garlic; discard garlic. Put wine and lemon juice into the pot and heat until bubbles rise to the top of the liquid. Add the cheese, about ⅓ of it at a time, stirring vigorously. When all the cheese is added, stir well, remove from heat. Taste and add salt and pepper. Transfer to lighted burner on the table. Have French bread ready in a basket for guests to spear and dunk into the cheese sauce. Serves 4 to 6.

Mandarin Salad

1 head crisp lettuce, chilled
1 sweet Bermuda onion, sliced, chilled
1 can (8 ounces) drained mandarin orange sections, halved
½ cup walnut halves
Italian Dressing (see below)

Tear lettuce into bite-size pieces and toss in salad bowl with onions and oranges. Top with the walnuts. Serve with Italian Dressing. Makes 4 to 6 servings.

Italian Dressing

1 teaspoon each salt and sugar
½ teaspoon celery salt
dash cayenne pepper
¼ teaspoon dry hot mustard
⅓ cup white wine vinegar
1 cup salad oil
1 clove garlic, minced or mashed
dash tabasco sauce

Combine all dressing ingredients in the blender or in a jar and process or shake until well blended. If you do this in a blender just before using it, the dressing will remain suspended longer. Makes about 1½ cups dressing.

American Trifle

4 *eggs, separated*
1 *cup sugar*
½ *cup flour*
1 *teaspoon baking powder*
¼ *teaspoon salt*
2 *teaspoons vanilla*
1 *cup diced, sugared dates (available commercially already diced and sugared)*
1 *cup chopped walnuts*
3 *bananas, diced*
1 *orange, peeled and diced*
1 *can (about 16 ounces) pitted black cherries, drained*
1 *can (about 15 ounces) crushed pineapple, drained*
½ *cup pineapple juice, reserved from crushed pineapple*
1 *cup cream, whipped*

Beat egg whites in small bowl of mixer until stiff. Set aside. Put egg yolks into large bowl and beat until creamy; gradually add the sugar and beat until fluffy. Stir in the flour, baking powder, salt, and vanilla until mixture is smooth. Blend in the whipped egg whites until well mixed. Fold in the dates and walnuts. Turn into a buttered 9- by 13-inch pan and bake in 350° oven for 30 minutes. Cool.

Blend the bananas, orange, cherries, and pineapple. Break the cake into bite-size pieces. Put ⅓ of the cake into the bottom of a pretty glass bowl. Top with half the fruit mixture. Top fruit with another ⅓ of the cake pieces. Top with remaining fruit mixture. Top fruit with the remaining cake pieces. Sprinkle cake with the reserved pineapple juice. Spread the whipped cream over the top of the whole thing. Refrigerate at least 2 hours before serving. Makes at least 6 servings.

※

A Teen-Age Apple-Dunking Fondue Party

※ Halloween could be in February as well as October for anybody with a good imagination. Who needs hobgoblins to dunk apple slices into a fondue pot? But then, with innovative young minds, who says that apples are all that can be dunked into cheese fondue (besides bread, of course)? Too bad young adults seem less innovative and experimental with food than they are with almost anything else! When taste buds are developed to appreciate new flavor combinations, each discovery can be a great event. This simple menu can be a pleasant surprise while teaching new flavor combination skills. By all means add to it if you find more foods that "go with" cheese fondue.

❀

Cider Cheese Fondue
Apple Slices   Pear Slices   Bread Chunks
Corn Chips (purchased, ready-made)
Sugar Cookies   Hot Fruited Tea

❀

About all you need to do to get this menu ready is to slice fruit, cube bread, and make the cider fondue. Sugar cookies are a simple matter, but if you prefer you might even buy them (from a *good* bakery, of course).

The tea is a dry mix that you make yourself, and you'll discover that it is convenient to keep on hand.

Cider Cheese Fondue

2 *pounds medium or sharp Cheddar cheese, according to your taste (we discovered that the unaged mild cheese can get stringy and be difficult to melt, so choose an aged, sharper Cheddar)*
2 *tablespoons cornstarch or flour*
1 *teaspoon dry mustard*
2 *cups apple cider*
2 *tablespoons butter*
salt and pepper to taste

For dipping: apple slices; pear slices; French bread in 1-inch cubes, each with some crust; Corn Chips, etc.

Cut cheese into ½-inch dice or shred it coarsely. Put into a bowl and add the cornstarch or flour and the mustard. Toss until the cheese pieces are thoroughly coated with the starch. In the cheese fondue pot, heat the apple cider to simmering. Add the butter. Add ⅓ of the cheese, stirring vigorously until it is melted, then add the remaining ⅔ a third at a time, stirring vigorously after each addition. Add salt and pepper to taste. Bring fondue to the serving table and place on lighted fondue burner. Have the fruit, bread, and Corn Chips in bowls around the table. Add whatever else you can think of for dunking. Makes 6 servings.

Simple Sugar Cookies

1 cup granulated sugar
1 cup powdered sugar
1 cup butter
1 cup salad oil
2 eggs
4½ cups flour
1 teaspoon salt
1 teaspoon soda
1 teaspoon cream of tartar

Cream the sugars with the butter. Add the oil, eggs, and flour along with the salt, soda, and cream of tartar. Blend together very well. Chill about 2 hours or until stiff. Shape into balls the size of walnuts. Put on an ungreased cooky sheet and flatten with a glass dipped in sugar. Bake for 8 minutes in 375° oven. Makes about 8 dozen.

Fruited Tea Mix

2 cups orange-flavored juice crystals
¾ cup instant tea with lemon and sugar
1 package (3 ounces) lemon-flavored gelatin dessert
1 package (3 ounces) orange-flavored gelatin dessert
1 cup sugar

Mix all ingredients together well and store in a tightly covered jar. Add 2 teaspoons of this mix and a stick of cinnamon to a cup of hot water to make a delightful fruit-flavored tea. Keeps well. Makes about 5 cups mix.

Fontina Americana Fondue

Here's a fondue that is ideal for a family meal. It's rich in all the nutrients that come from milk and milk products. There is a classic version of this fondue that is prepared in Switzerland using real Emmentaler. However, for family use, we've adapted the idea to the use of domestic cheeses.

The flavors are very good, and if you choose to serve it to gourmets, add dry red claret to the menu as a refreshing contrast to the richly flavored fontina.

*

Fontina Americana Fondue
Crusty Bread Chunks, Italian or French
Apricot-Orange Salad Mold
Soft Drinks or Grapefruit Juice
Brown Sugar—Nutmeg Fruit Bake

*

Make the salad the day before and assemble the dessert 24 hours ahead of time, too. All you have to do at dinnertime is cut up the cheese and make the fondue.

Fontina Americana Fondue

½ pound white brick cheese or white Cheddar
½ pound aged domestic Swiss cheese or Baby Swiss (aged over 90 days)
4 tablespoons flour
2 cups milk
dash salt
½ teaspoon hot dry mustard
dash nutmeg
1 loaf French bread, cut in 1-inch pieces
cherry tomatoes
smoked sausage links (optional)

Cut the cheese into ½-inch cubes or coarsely grate and put into a bowl. Add the flour and toss until cheese pieces are thoroughly coated. Heat milk in cheese fondue pot to simmering. Add the floured cheese ⅓ at a time and stir vigorously until the cheese is melted; add the remaining ⅔ of the flour ⅓ at a time, stirring vigorously. Add the salt and nutmeg to taste. Bring to the table and place on lighted fondue burner. Guests spear chunks of French bread, cherry tomatoes, or sausages (if you choose to serve them), and swirl into the melted cheese. Makes 4 to 6 servings.

Apricot-Orange Salad Mold

½ cup water
1½ cups apricot juice
1 package (3 ounces) lemon-flavored gelatin
1 package (3 ounces) cream cheese
1 can (8 ounces) mandarin oranges, drained
1 cup whipping cream, whipped

Combine juice and water and bring to a boil. Add gelatin and stir until dissolved. Cool until thickened. Cream the cheese and beat into the gelatin. Arrange orange slices in a salad mold and pour gelatin mixture over them. Refrigerate until set, preferably overnight. Makes 4 to 6 servings.

Brown Sugar–Nutmeg Fruit Bake

1 *can (about 8 ounces) peach halves, drained*
1 *can (about 8 ounces) sliced pineapple, drained*
1 *can (about 8 ounces) pear halves, drained*
5 *maraschino cherries, drained*
¼ *cup butter*
⅓ *cup light brown sugar, well packed*
1 *teaspoon nutmeg*

Drain fruit on paper towels. Arrange in a casserole or a 9-inch-square baking pan. Melt the butter, add the brown sugar and nutmeg. Spoon over the fruit. Refrigerate for 24 hours. Bake in 350° oven for 30 minutes before serving. Serve with whipped cream, if desired. Makes about 6 servings.

Welsh Rabbit, Fondue Style

❂ Sometimes this is called a "rarebit," sometimes "rabbit." I like rabbit better. I suppose the authentic dish varies a little from one Welsh home to another. Maybe that's what makes a traditional dish identifiable with a certain area of the world—it can vary from home to home yet be identified by a specific name.

Welsh Rabbit is an ideal meal for a family. It's simple and nourishing, and because of the wide price range of different cheeses, it can be quite inexpensive.

Because there's such a natural affinity to fresh vegetables, we're suggesting that you dip fresh vegetables into the rabbit instead of pouring the rabbit onto toast, which is the classic way to serve it. So, for a family meal, rabbit becomes well balanced as well. And, best of all, it tastes good.

Classically, the cheese used for a Welsh Rabbit is supposed to be a sharp Cheddar. The liquid used should be a "stale ale." No reason why *you* couldn't use a milder Cheddar if you prefer, or milk or apple juice for the liquid if that's more acceptable to your palate.

Besides being great for a family meal, this is a terrific dunk for those television viewers who must munch. Let them munch a meal. Or serve Welsh Rabbit after a sporting event, a play or a movie, or even an opera.

❋

Welsh Rabbit, Fondue Style

Rye Breadsticks Celery Sticks Carrot Sticks
Zucchini Sticks Turnip Sticks
Apple Wedges Cherry Tomatoes Cauliflowerets
Ale or Burgundy
Coffee Fresh Fruit
Sesame Seed Butter Crisps and Ginger Crisps

❋

Make the rye breadsticks at any time in advance and store them in the freezer or in an airtight container. Cut up the vegetables in advance and keep them in an airtight plastic container or bag, refrigerated; pile them into bowls for serving. Make the Welsh Rabbit five minutes before you are ready to serve your meal.

Welsh Rabbit, Fondue Style

3 tablespoons flour
3 tablespoons butter
½ cup milk
1 cup ale
1 pound diced sharp Cheddar cheese
½ teaspoon salt
¼ cup sherry
dash tabasco sauce

Blend the flour into the butter and heat in a saucepan, stirring while you add the milk and ale. Heat slowly, stirring until thickened. Remove from the heat and stir in the cheese, blending until smooth. Add the salt and sherry, stirring until blended. Heat slowly until bubbling. Add tabasco for flavoring. Bring to the table and place on lighted fondue burner. Serve with assorted dunkables as given in the menu. Makes about 4 servings.

Rye Breadsticks

1 *package active dry yeast*
⅓ *cup lukewarm water*
⅔ *cup rye meal*
1⅓ *cups sifted all-purpose flour*
1 *teaspoon salt*
1 *teaspoon sugar*
3 *tablespoons salad oil*
¼ *cup warm milk*

Soften the yeast in the water. Combine this mixture with the rye meal. Beat well. Let rise until double in bulk (about 1 hour). Sift the remaining flour with the salt and sugar and add along with the oil and milk to the first mixture. Knead thoroughly on a lightly floured board. Place in lightly greased bowl; cover. Let dough rise until doubled. Knead again until bubbles are out and divide into three equal parts. Divide each part into 12 pieces. Roll each piece of dough on a lightly floured board into strips about 4 inches long. Place them about an inch apart on a greased baking sheet. Brush with milk, and bake in 400° oven for 12 minutes or until golden. Let cool and store in a tightly covered container until ready to use. Makes 3 dozen.

Sesame Seed Butter Crisps

1 *teaspoon butter*
½ *cup sesame seeds*
¾ *cup (1½ sticks) butter*
1½ *cups brown sugar, firmly packed*
2 *eggs*
1½ *cups sifted flour*
½ *teaspoon baking powder*
¼ *teaspoon salt*
1 *teaspoon vanilla*

Melt 1 teaspoon butter in a frying pan over low heat. Add the sesame seeds and stir until all are golden brown; set aside. Cream together the ¾ cup of butter with the brown sugar until light. Beat in the eggs. Sift flour with the baking powder and salt into the creamed mixture. Add the vanilla and toasted sesame seeds. Drop by teaspoonfuls onto a lightly greased and floured cooky sheet. Bake in 325° oven for about 15 minutes or until lightly browned. Remove cookies from pan immediately and cool on a rack. Makes about 5 dozen.

Ginger Crisps

½ *cup dark molasses*
¼ *cup butter*
1¾ *cups sifted flour*
¼ *teaspoon soda*
1½ *teaspoons ground ginger*
½ *teaspoon salt*

Put molasses and butter into pan and heat until butter is melted. Add the flour, soda, ginger, and salt; mix well and chill thoroughly. Roll out a small portion of the dough at a time on a well-floured board. Dough must be rolled out paper-thin. Cut into 2-inch circles and bake on a greased cooky sheet in 350° oven for 6 minutes or until cookies just begin to brown. They will be very crisp if you've rolled the dough out thin enough. Makes about 100 cookies.

Fondue with Italian Flavors

☀ Spaghetti and meatball fans might enjoy this change of pace menu. It's a fondue based on cooking things in oil—so you'll use your beef fondue pot. There's lots of eating in the total menu, and it is fun. You might want to eliminate some items, though; to simplify or make it less filling is your choice. A simpler menu could omit the tomato sauce and the spaghetti. You could substitute bought breadsticks for the *grissini*. But that's an awfully good recipe, and making them yourself is a great satisfaction.

This menu requires considerable make-ahead activity. Make the Grissini ahead and keep them stored in an airtight container. Shape the Parmesan Balls and Steak Balls early in the day and keep them chilled. The Tomato Sauce and the Salsa Verde can be made either early in the day, or the day before, if you wish.

The Almond Tortoni must be frozen, so you should make it the day before. Cook the spaghetti just before serving time and dress it with oil and garlic.

❈

Fondue Roma

Parmesan Balls   Salisbury Steak Balls
Tomato Sauce   Salsa Verde
Spaghetti with Oil and Garlic   Italian Cauliflower Salad
Grissini
Almond Tortoni

❈

Fondue Roma

Parmesan Balls:

1½ cups fresh bread crumbs	2 teaspoons minced parsley
2 cups grated Parmesan cheese	3 eggs, lightly beaten
½ teaspoon salt	8 ounces mozzarella cheese,
¼ teaspoon pepper	diced in ¾-inch cubes
dash nutmeg	1 egg, beaten

Salisbury Steak Balls:

1 pound Salisbury steaks or ground round steak	¼ teaspoon coarsely ground pepper
1 teaspoon salt	
2 to 3 cups cooking oil for fondue pot	

To make the Parmesan Balls, blend 1 cup of the bread crumbs with the Parmesan cheese, salt, pepper, nutmeg, parsley, and the 3 beaten eggs. Shape about 1 tablespoon of the mixture around each cube of mozzarella cheese, making a perfect ball. Dip in beaten egg and roll in the remaining bread crumbs. Refrigerate until serving time. At the table, spear each ball with a fondue fork and cook in the hot oil until browned (about 1 minute). For the Salisbury steak balls, blend the meat with the salt and pepper and shape into balls no more than 1 inch in diameter. Arrange on a tray and at the table spear each one with a fondue fork, cook in the hot oil, and eat with the sauces provided. Heat the oil in the fondue pot to about 375° before bringing it to the table, and place on lighted burner.

Have no more than four people per fondue pot. If you are serving six people with this menu, provide two pots. Fondue Roma will serve four to six persons, depending on appetites.

Tomato Sauce

2 *tablespoons butter*
3 *large ripe tomatoes, peeled, seeded, and chopped*
1 *teaspoon* each *sugar and salt*
½ *teaspoon sweet basil*
1 *tablespoon Cognac or brandy or white cooking wine*

Melt butter in pan and add the tomatoes, sugar, salt, and basil. Simmer until smooth and thickened (about 20 minutes). Add the Cognac or brandy. Serve hot or cold. Makes about 2 cups. Refrigerate any remaining portions; it will keep about a week.

Salsa Verde

¾ *cup minced fresh parsley*
1½ *tablespoons chopped capers (optional)*
1½ *tablespoons chopped dill pickle*
1 *small clove garlic, mashed*
1 *slice white bread, crusts removed*
⅛ *teaspoon freshly ground pepper*
¼ *teaspoon salt*
pinch sugar
¼ *cup olive oil*
¼ *cup red or white wine vinegar*

Combine all ingredients in blender, giving it four on-off whirls at low speed, just enough to chop the ingredients into a coarse sauce. Or, beat in small bowl using electric mixer until all ingredients are blended. Makes about 1½ cups sauce.

Spaghetti with Oil and Garlic

1 pound thin spaghetti
6 quarts water, boiling
2 teaspoons salt
1 tablespoon salad oil
½ cup olive oil
3 cloves garlic, minced or mashed
½ cup finely minced fresh parsley
½ to 1 cup freshly grated Parmesan or Romano cheese
    (optional)

Put the spaghetti into boiling water; add the salt and boil for 6 minutes. Add the 1 tablespoon salad oil, and cook for 2 minutes more. Drain and pour into a heated serving dish.

Meanwhile, in a saucepan, heat the olive oil until hot but not boiling; add the garlic and let stand off the heat for about one minute. Then add the parsley; stir immediately into the hot spaghetti and serve. Offer additional grated Parmesan cheese, if desired. Makes 4 to 6 generous servings.

Italian Cauliflower Salad

1 meduim-size head cauliflower
½ teaspoon salt
¼ teaspoon freshly ground pepper
2 tablespoons vinegar
5 tablespoons olive oil
1 tablespoon capers
1 teaspoon minced fresh parsley
12 chopped black olives
1 small head romaine, washed, leaves broken apart

Wash the cauliflower and break apart into flowerets. Drop into boiling salted water and cook for about 7 minutes, or until tender crisp, not soft. Drain, rinse in cold water, and chill. Combine the salt, pepper, vinegar, oil, capers, parsley, and olives and blend the mixture into the flowerets. Arrange on a bed of romaine and serve. Makes 6 servings.

Grissini

1 package active dry yeast
⅓ cup warm water
2 cups unsifted all-purpose flour
1 teaspoon salt
1 teaspoon sugar
3 tablespoons salad oil
¼ cup warm milk

Dissolve the yeast in the water. Add 1 cup of the flour and knead for 5 minutes. Cover, and let rise in a warm place until double in bulk (about 1 hour). Sift the remaining flour with the salt and sugar and add to the risen mixture along with the oil and milk. Knead thoroughly. Cover again and let rise until double in bulk (about 1½ hours). Turn dough out onto a lightly floured board and divide into three equal sections. Divide each section into 12 parts. Each will be the size of a walnut. Roll each part out on breadboard into strips about 4 inches long. Place an inch apart on greased baking sheets and let rise for 30 minutes. Brush with milk and bake in 400° oven for 12 minutes or until golden. Let cool. Store in a tightly covered container. Makes 36.

Almond Tortoni

2 egg whites
⅔ cup powdered sugar
2 cups whipping cream
1 cup crushed dry almond macaroons
2 tablespoons rum
½ cup chopped toasted almonds

Beat egg whites until stiff; add ⅓ cup of the powdered sugar and continue beating until powdered sugar is well blended in and mixture resembles a meringue. Beat the cream until thick; add the remaining ⅓ cup powdered sugar and continue beating until stiff. Fold the crushed macaroons and the rum into the whipped cream. Fold the egg whites into the cream well. Pour into 8 fluted paper cups or cupcake liners. Sprinkle top with chopped toasted almonds. Put the tortoni into the freezer until firm. Wrap well to keep foreign flavors away from the tortoni. Makes 8.

Fondue with Pizza Flavors

There are many times for most of us mothers when we're left to serve the kids' dinner when dad's gone somewhere. To come up with something that they really enjoy other than hamburgers and hot dogs can sometimes demand genius. Many children enjoy fondue because it is an "activity" type of meal.

This fondue is basically a cheese sauce that has all the flavors of pizza right in the fondue pot. You dunk bread chunks and chunks of iceberg lettuce right into it. The menu is light and uncomplicated. When dad is home, you might invite a couple of friends over and serve this fondue as an appetizer.

If you feel ambitious, you could make your own bread using the yeast and flour from two pizza mixes. Just follow the directions on the package to make pizza crust, being sure to knead the dough well, shape into long loaves French-bread style, let rise, and bake in 375° oven for 20 to 25 minutes or until the bread is nice and crusty. Then dunk pieces of bread in the Pizza Cheese Fondue.

✿

Pizza Cheese Fondue
Bread Chunks   Iceberg Lettuce Chunks
Peanut Butter Brownies

✿

Pizza Cheese Fondue

 1 medium-size onion, finely chopped
 ½ pound ground round steak
 2 tablespoons butter or oil
 2 cups (two 8-ounce cans) prepared tomato sauce or pizza sauce
 3 tablespoons flour
1½ teaspoons anise seed or fennel seed
 1 teaspoon each oregano and basil
 ¼ teaspoon garlic powder
 ¼ cup grated Parmesan cheese
 ½ pound (8 ounces) Cheddar cheese (mild, medium, or sharp) shredded
 1 cup shredded mozzarella cheese
crusty bread chunks
iceberg lettuce chunks

In the cheese fondue pot, brown the onion and the meat in the butter over medium heat. Break meat apart so that it is fine and crumbly. Add the tomato sauce and bring to a boil. Meanwhile, blend the flour, anise seed, oregano, garlic powder, Parmesan cheese, Cheddar cheese, and mozzarella cheese together well, until all cheese is lightly coated with flour. Add a small portion at a time of the cheese mixture to the sauce, stir until it is melted. Fold in the remaining cheese mixture. Mixture will be quite thick. Remove from heat before cheese is entirely melted and transfer fondue pot to lighted burner set at low heat. (Beware the dangers of a flaming burner around children!) Don't stir the fondue too much before you bring it to the table; when the mozzarella cheese melts, it becomes stringy. Mozzarella adds a delightful authentic flavor, nevertheless. Dip chunks of bread and lettuce into the fondue to eat it. Makes four generous servings, or will serve up to eight youngsters, depending on appetites.

Peanut Butter Brownies

½ *cup butter*
2 *squares unsweetened baking chocolate*
1 *cup sugar*
2 *eggs, unbeaten*
½ *cup flour*
½ *teaspoon baking powder*
½ *cup chopped walnuts*
1 *teaspoon vanilla*
½ *cup soft peanut butter*
One Minute Fudge Frosting (see below)

Melt butter and chocolate together in a saucepan. Add the sugar and the eggs and beat well. Sift the flour and baking powder together into the pan and blend well. Add the nuts and vanilla. Spread in a buttered 8-inch-square pan and bake in 350° oven for 30 minutes or until brownies shrink away from the edge of the pan. Spread with the peanut butter, then with the fudge frosting while still hot. Cut into 12 squares.

One Minute Fudge Frosting

1 *square (1 ounce) unsweetened chocolate*
1 *cup sugar*
¼ *cup butter*
⅓ *cup milk*
½ *teaspoon salt*
vanilla

Blend all ingredients except the vanilla together in a saucepan and bring to a boil after the chocolate has melted. Boil 1 minute. Cool and add the vanilla. Beat until thick enough to spread.

Cheese Fondue with Mexican Flavors

✹ Mexican Chili con Queso (chili with cheese) is one of my favorite dips. It's a delight to serve for a brunch, lunch, or a light supper along with Corn Chips or Tostaditas. This makes a great cocktail dip, too, if you're interested in something different to serve for appetizers.

This menu is designed to be a brunch or lunch suggestion.

✿

Cheese Fondue with Mexican Flavors
Fresh Papaya with Lime
Chili Con Queso   Tostaditas
Pan Dulce   Mexican Chocolate

✿

Start this brunch or lunch with a quartered papaya topped with a slice of fresh lime. Squeeze the lime juice onto the papaya first. This course is cleared away and then you bring in the Chili con Queso and the Tostaditas. You can have the Chili con Queso waiting for you in the kitchen on no heat at all. Let it reheat slowly over the fondue burner. Guests dip the Tostaditas into the peppery cheese sauce. The Pan Dulce, a Mexican sweet bread, is very nice made into tiny buns to serve with the Mexican chocolate for dessert.

Chili Con Queso

1 small onion, finely minced (about ¼ cup)
2 tablespoons butter
1 can (8 ounces) solid pack tomatoes
1 can (4 ounces) peeled, chopped green chilies
1 package (8 ounces) cream cheese, cubed
1 cup light cream
salt and pepper to taste

Sauté the onion in the butter until onion is soft but not browned. Add the tomatoes and chilies and simmer for 15 minutes. Add the cheese and stir until it begins to melt. Add the cream. Taste and add salt and pepper. Makes 4 servings.

Tostaditas

12 cornmeal tortillas
oil for deep frying

Cut the tortillas into 16 wedges each, using a pair of scissors. Heat oil to 375° to 400°, drop tortilla wedges into the oil, and fry until crisp and golden. Remove from hot fat and drain thoroughly on paper toweling. Keep in an airtight container or plastic bag so they will not soften until you're ready to use them. Tostaditas may be prepared the day before you plan to serve the Chili con Queso. Spare ones may be stored for later use. Makes about 200.

Pan Dulce (Mexican Sweet Bread)

1 package active dry yeast
½ cup warm water
½ cup sugar
1 teaspoon salt
2 tablespoons melted shortening or oil
2 eggs, beaten
3½ cups sifted all-purpose flour
Crunch Topping (see below)

Dissolve the yeast in the warm water. Let stand 5 minutes, then stir. Add the sugar, salt, shortening, and eggs, mixing well. Stir in half the flour and beat well. Cover and let rise in a warm place until dough is bubbly and about double in bulk. Add the remaining flour, stirring until a stiff dough is formed. Knead until smooth. Put into a lightly greased bowl; cover and let rise for 1 hour. Divide dough into quarters. Divide each quarter into 4 parts. Then divide the resulting pieces of dough into 4 pieces again. You will have 64 pieces of dough. Form each into a round flat bun. Spread each with the Crunch Topping. Place on lightly greased cooky sheet and let rise until double in bulk, about 1 hour. Bake in 400° oven for about 15 minutes or until golden. Makes 64 tiny buns. (These are delightful served with butter and marmalade.)

Crunch Topping

½ cup sugar
¼ cup shortening
¼ teaspoon salt
1 teaspoon cinnamon
1 egg yolk
⅔ cup sifted all-purpose flour

Blend together all ingredients until a crumbly mixture results.

Mexican Chocolate

6 cups milk
1 package (6 ounces) sweet chocolate
dash cinnamon

Heat milk slowly and add the chocolate, broken into squares; stir until chocolate is melted. Then with a Mexican chocolate stick (called a molinillo) beat the chocolate vigorously until it foams. If you do not have a molinillo, use a rotary beater, beating until chocolate has a nice layer of foam on top. Makes 6 cups.

✹

Television Viewer's Snack Fondue

✹ Here's a fondue that will bring some good nutri-
tion into those who are glued to the television program, be it
football, baseball, or moon walks. The fondue we're presenting
here has favorite flavors right in it—onions, cheese, and tomato
juice. Dippables include vegetable sticks, corn chips, and/or
French or rye bread cubes. For dessert, offer a bowl of brightly
polished apples.

❉

Onion-Cheese Fondue
Corn Chips   Vegetable Sticks   Bread Cubes
Fresh Apples

❉

Prepare a variety of fresh vegetables of your choice, such as celery sticks, carrot sticks, zucchini sticks, cucumber sticks, tomato wedges, or whatever is a favorite and handy. Pile them all in a bowl. Chill until serving time. Put corn chips into another bowl, bread cubes into still another. Provide toothpicks and/or fondue forks. You can get by without any plates at all if you play it right. Serve the beverage of your choice.

Onion-Cheese Fondue

2 cups tomato juice or vegetable juice
2 tablespoons lemon juice
1 envelope (about 1¼ ounces) onion soup mix
1 pound processed American cheese, diced into ½-inch pieces
1 tablespoon flour

Combine tomato juice, lemon juice, and onion soup mix in a cheese fondue pot or caquelon. Toss the cheese and flour together until cheese cubes are lightly dusted with the flour. Bring liquid in pot to simmering and add a small portion of the cheese at a time, stirring until cheese is melted. Continue adding cheese after each addition is melted until all cheese is used and fondue is smooth and thick. Guests spear bread cubes and dip into the fondue, or dip vegetables or corn chips into the pot to eat. Makes about 6 servings.

❊

After-Theatre Fondue for Six

❊ Having the best recipes in town does not qualify you as a good cook, nor does being able to produce good dishes make you one. The secret of good cooking lies in making the perfect selection of food for each occasion, and choosing just the right combination of textures and tastes to serve together. How many times have you encountered a meal that involved so many dishes you really didn't have a chance to enjoy a particular one? Or, how often have you been tempted to plan a menu of all your favorite dishes—the soup, a salad, the main dish, a favorite bread, dessert, and so forth—all rolled into one menu. They don't necessarily come off as well as when you select one and complement it with subordinates of high quality, perfectly prepared, that don't mask the flavor or compete with the appeal of the *pièce de ré-*

sistance. In other words, you need only one "superstar" in each menu you prepare.

This seafood-cheese fondue is that kind of superstar, a specialty that makes an appealing after-theatre experience. The bouilla-baisse fondue is not too heavy and goes well with foods that are light and refreshing and offer pleasing contrasts. You might enjoy trying it some evening after entertainment with two or four good friends.

Serve a chilled crisp white Burgundy or chilled champagne.

✿

Bouillabaisse Fondue
Crusty French Bread Cubes
Garden Lettuce Salad   Lemon Butter Dressing
Raspberry Soufflé Froid

✿

To prepare the meal, you do most of the work before you leave for the theatre. You need only to reheat the fondue to bubbling, add the cheese and place it on a lighted fondue burner on the table. Heat the dressing for the salad, which should be prepared ahead and kept covered in the refrigerator. At the very last (even after you've all been seated), you may pour the hot dressing over the salad. The dessert is actually a chilled mousse that you make the day before or very early in the day so that it has time to set.

Bouillabaisse Fondue

 2 *cans (10 ounces each) cream of shrimp soup, thawed*
 1 *cup dry white wine*
 ½ *pound cooked frozen shrimp, thawed under cold water*
 ½ *pound lobster tails, cooked, shelled and chunked*
 ½ *pound scallops, thawed*
 2 *cups coarsely shredded Swiss cheese, aged 90 days or more*
 2 *tablespoons flour*
paprika
lemon wedges (optional)

To prepare the fondue ahead, combine the shrimp soup, wine, shrimp, shelled lobster tails, and scallops in fondue pot. Cover and leave in the refrigerator until serving time. Have the cheese blended with the flour in a bowl at room temperature. When you're ready to eat, put pot on medium flame, stir until mixture is warmed and will stir easily, raise heat to high, and cook until bubbly. Add the Swiss cheese in two portions, stirring until it is melted. Top with a dash of paprika and place pot on lighted fondue burner at the table. Guests spear cubes of French bread and dip into the sauce. They use their fondue forks to fish out pieces of seafood. Provide extra lemon wedges, if desired. Makes 6 servings.

Garden Lettuce Salad

1 head romaine
1 head chicory
1 head Boston or Bibb lettuce

Wash, drain, and separate all leaves of lettuce, dry carefully. Leave lettuce leaves whole. Toss in a wooden bowl at the table with Lemon Butter Dressing. Makes 6 servings.

Lemon Butter Dressing

2 tablespoons lemon juice
¼ teaspoon pepper
6 tablespoons butter

Combine ingredients. Heat slowly to bubbling; mix well with fork. Drizzle over lettuce and toss. Makes ½ cup dressing.

Raspberry Soufflé Froid

5 egg yolks
½ cup sugar
1 package (10 ounces) frozen
raspberries, thawed

2 envelopes unflavored gelatin
½ cup Kirschwasser
5 egg whites
1 cup heavy cream, whipped

Beat the egg yolks and sugar together until thick and pale in color. Takes about 5 minutes at high speed with electric mixer. Meanwhile strain juice from frozen raspberries, measure, and add water to equal 1¼ cups. Blend ½ cup of the raspberry juice and water mixture with the gelatin; set over hot water to dissolve. Blend remaining juice mixture and the Kirschwasser into the dissolved gelatin mixture and beat into the egg yolk and sugar mixture, whipping it in well. Chill until just syrupy.

Whip the egg whites until stiff and fold into the gelatin mixture. Fold in the whipped cream and the raspberries. Butter a soufflé dish about 1 quart size and tie a standing collar of waxed paper around the edge. Turn the raspberry mixture into the dish and chill until set (at least 8 hours). Decorate the top with additional whipped cream, if desired. Makes 6 servings.

Japanese Sukiyaki, Fondue Style

This classic dish is less a "fondue" than most others we've talked about so far. But, since you should cook it at the table and serve yourself from a common vessel, we're including it here among the fondues. Sukiyaki should be cooked over a high direct flame. It cooks quickly and is really best when a small amount is cooked at a time. This makes sukiyaki especially adaptable to fondue-style eating. Put a shallow blazer pan (such as the upper part of a chafing dish that holds food) over a burner—don't use the bottom pan that's meant to contain the water. Then have your guests at the table cook small portions of their own meat and vegetables quickly in a small amount of fat, cooking several portions throughout the meal.

✿

Japanese Beef Sukiyaki
Fluffy White Rice
Warm Sake   Tea
Fresh Fruit Compote

✿

To get the meal ready, slice the uncooked beef and raw vegetables thin and arrange on a serving tray. Toss together the fresh fruit compote and chill it. Cook the rice at the last, prepare the tea, and warm the sake. Provide chopsticks for people to cook with and to eat with.

Japanese Beef Sukiyaki

2 *pounds beef sirloin or tenderloin, very thinly sliced to about 2- by 3-inch pieces*
4 *stalks celery, sliced diagonally about ¼ inch thick*
1 *bunch green onions, cleaned, cut into 1-inch pieces diagonally*
½ *pound fresh mushrooms, cleaned, thinly sliced*
½ *pound fresh spinach leaves, washed, cut into ½-inch strips*
1 *can (16 ounces) bean sprouts, drained and washed in ice water*
½ *pound tofu (bean curd), if available, cut into 1-inch cubes*
cooking oil in small pitcher
cooking broth (see below)

Arrange sliced meat and vegetables attractively on serving trays. Cover and refrigerate until serving time. At the table, heat pan and add a small amount of cooking oil, just enough to moisten the bottom of the pan. Pass meat and vegetables around. Each guest selects his own and places them in a pile in the skillet, cooking his own batch of sukiyaki. Have cooking broth in a pitcher. Pour over all six batches of meat and vegetables. Simmer until vegetables are tender crisp.

Meanwhile pass around the fluffy rice and the sake and tea. Put cooked sukiyaki on a portion of rice, put more in to cook, and while the second batch is cooking enjoy your first batch. Makes about 6 servings.

Sukiyaki Cooking Broth

½ *cup Japanese style soy sauce*
2 *tablespoons sugar*
¼ *cup sake or dry sherry*
1 *cup beef broth*
½ *cup water*

Blend soy sauce, sugar, sake or dry sherry, beef broth, and water. Stir well. Pour into pitcher to bring to the table. Makes about 2 cups.

Fluffy White Rice

1½ *cups long grain rice*
½ *teaspoon salt*
3 *cups boiling water*

Add rice and salt to boiling water gradually to keep water at boiling stage. Stir with a fork, cover, lower heat, and let stand for 20 minutes without removing cover. Rice will have absorbed all the liquid, and needs only to be fluffed with a fork and served immediately. Makes 6 servings.

Fresh Fruit Compote

1 *can (8 ounces) mandarin orange sections, drained*
2 *cups diced fresh pineapple*
¼ *cup finely minced maraschino cherries*
1 *fresh pear, peeled and diced*
2 *tablespoons Kirschwasser, brandy, or Cognac*

Blend orange sections with the pineapple, cherries, and pear. Pour the liqueur flavoring over all, stir, cover, and refrigerate until ready to serve. Makes 6 servings.

Oriental Firepot, Fondue Style

The Mongolian or Oriental firepot is a fascinating piece of equipment to own. It's a conversation piece in itself, and if you have one it should be displayed and used as an ornamental item in your home, not stuck on a storage shelf somewhere. Of course, it adds to the conversational value of the pot if you *do* use it occasionally.

The menu we're suggesting here is not only "just" to use the firepot, but also to show how you can use your regular fondue pot for something new. Firepot cooking is essentially cooking in a rich broth rather than in oil. The resulting food is delectable, and the special sauce you use on the cooked food has a characteristic flavor all its own, also delicious.

One of the first things you wonder about when you think of using the Oriental firepot is how to fire it. We tried using an alcohol burner, a sterno can, candles. They were all unsatisfactory. The *only* way is to fire up some charcoal briquettes and place them in the compartment intended for them beneath the broth vessel. The charcoals (it will take six or eight of them) will keep the vessel hot for about an hour. You need to stoke it up again when the broth seems to lose its heat. This is not hard to do, and, surprisingly, doesn't fill your dining room with smoke.

The meal goes like this: The diner chooses a selection of raw meat and vegetables from the platter (or platters). He puts a selection of them into the hot pot just in front of him. Everybody does this at once. You then can put the lid on the moat and let it cook for 3 to 5 minutes. Meanwhile, sip sake, and pass around the rice. Then, you remove your food from the moat and put more in. While the second batch is cooking, dip the cooked food in sauces and eat it with rice. It's the most fun if you insist that everybody use chopsticks.

After about the second batch of meat and vegetables is cooked, ladle out the broth into soup cups, replace the broth (from supply kept in the kitchen), and enjoy the soup while another batch of vegetables and meats is cooking. This ritual can continue on just as long as the diners have the capacity.

As you can see, the firepot is a slow and relaxed way of eating. There's plenty of opportunity for laughter, experimentation, stories, and plain fun.

❀

Oriental Firepot Fondue

Fluffy Rice   *Condiments*
Warm Sake   *Hot Tea*
Almond Cookies

❀

Preparation: Select the meats and seafood you plan to serve, allowing 2 pounds total for 6 persons. For the cooking broth you may use about 5 quarts of rich chicken stock, or use the recipe we give in this menu (it's expensive, but *very* good). Select the condiments from the list, providing a minimum of two or three and a maximum according to your own taste and findings. You'll cook the rice at the last minute (see recipe in menu for sukiyaki on page 137). You can make the almond cookies or buy them.

You will need some large flat trays for arranging the sliced meat, seafood, and vegetables (they probably won't all fit on one).

To set the table you should provide a plate, soup bowl, teacup, sake cup, soup spoon, pair of chopsticks, and an extra bowl for the dipping sauce for each person. Other condiments can be spooned onto the dinner plate.

Oriental Firepot Fondue

For 6 people select 2 pounds of the following:

beef tenderloin or sirloin
boneless chicken breast
lean ham

cleaned raw shrimp
lobster, sliced
oysters

For 6 people select 5 or 6 of the following vegetables:

iceberg lettuce, cut in 2-inch squares
fresh spinach, cleaned, cut in ½-inch strips
snow peas, fresh or frozen, thawed
cucumbers, peeled and thinly sliced

fresh mushrooms, quartered or sliced
bamboo shoots, thinly sliced
water chestnuts, thinly sliced
Bok Choy, cut diagonally into ½-inch pieces
celery, cut diagonally into ½-inch pieces

Cooking Broth (see recipe below)
Dipping Sauce (see recipe below)

Select meats and vegetables you plan to include. Slice the beef, chicken, or ham thinly and arrange slices overlapping evenly on a serving tray. Leave shrimp and oysters whole, but slice the lobster into about ½-inch pieces and arrange on a tray. Prepare the vegetables as indicated above, arrange on a tray, cover trays with plastic wrap and refrigerate until serving time.

Meanwhile prepare the cooking broth (or use canned chicken broth, about 5 quarts in all), prepare the dipping sauce and have it ready.

To serve the Firepot Fondue, light about a dozen charcoal briquettes in a coffee can (holes punched in the bottom for air). When glowing, place into compartment on Oriental Firepot intended for the charcoal. Pour about 2½ quarts of boiling hot cooking broth into the moat. Cover. When guests are ready, remove cover, pass around meats, fish, and vegetables. The guests cook their own selected variety in the broth, cooking several pieces at a time. Meanwhile, pass around the condiments (dipping sauce should be provided in individual small bowls or cups), and pass around the rice.

About halfway through the meal, ladle out the broth and serve. Refill the moat with more boiling broth from the kitchen. Continue cooking vegetables and meat. The broth is supposed to be served twice, but it's been our experience that people are too full for another helping. (It makes a great soup the next day.)

Firepot Cooking Broth

5 quarts water
1 whole chicken
1 ham bone
1 pound lean pork, may be bony
1 can (8 ounces) minced clams
1 can (8 ounces) frozen oysters, thawed
salt to taste

Bring water to a boil in a large pot. Add the chicken, ham bone, and pork. Simmer for 1½ hours. Remove chicken, bone it, and save the meat for another use. Do the same with the ham bone and pork roast. Add the canned minced clams and oysters, broth and all, and simmer for 15 minutes more. Strain the whole thing, discarding bones and other particles. Return stock to the pot; taste and add salt. Add water to equal 5 quarts.

Condiments for Firepot Fondue

Choose from:

Japanese soy sauce

sherry and cornstarch (guests dip meat first into sherry then into the cornstarch before cooking)

hot Chinese mustard

freshly chopped green onions

grated fresh ginger root (see index)

Sesame Paste, Hoisin Sauce, Oyster Sauce (all are available in stores that handle imported Oriental foods), guests use these dips after cooking

teriyaki sauce, generally available

chutney, homemade or bought

Almond Cookies

The original recipe for these cookies calls for lard instead of butter, but I think butter gives them a better taste.

1 cup butter

1 cup sugar

1 egg

10 unblanched whole almonds, ground

1 teaspoon almond extract

2½ cups sifted all-purpose flour

1½ teaspoons baking powder

⅛ teaspoon salt

35 blanched whole almonds

Cream the butter and sugar in a mixing bowl until light. Beat in the egg and ground almonds. Add the almond extract, blending well. Sift flour, baking powder, and salt together and add gradually to the creamed mixture. If necessary add a few drops of water to make dough more workable. Roll out to ½-inch thickness on a lightly floured board. Cut out 1½-inch-diameter circles. Place on a lightly greased baking sheet. Press a whole blanched almond into the top of each cooky. Bake until golden in 350° oven about 15 minutes.

A Fondue Orientale Menu

This menu is a combination of ideas. It incorporates the method of cooking in broth (as firepot cooking does), with the simplicity of the original beef fondue. All you cook in the broth is meat. No vegetables. This is ideal for the beef fondue pot, although you could use the Oriental firepot or your cheese fondue pot.

❖

Fondue Orientale
Red Sauce   Sesame Sauce
Fluffy Rice   Cucumber Salad
Bananas in Silk Thread
Fortune Cookies

❖

To prepare the meal, cut up the meat and arrange it on a tray. Make your own beef broth or use canned broth. Make the Red Sauce and Sesame Sauce in advance, also the Cucumber Salad. Cook the rice just before serving. The dessert is a classic Oriental one that is fun to do. If you don't feel like being so ambitious, substitute plain bananas with cream and sugar. We're giving a recipe for Fortune Cookies here, because some people really enjoy trying things like this. If you don't, just buy your Fortune Cookies.

Fondue Orientale

½ pound beef tenderloin or sirloin per person, thinly sliced (or
    chicken breast, pork tenderloin, lamb or veal)
3 cups rich beef broth or chicken broth

Arrange sliced meat on a tray; don't season before cooking or broth will be very salty. Put broth into fondue pot and heat to boiling in the kitchen, bring to the table and keep at a rolling boil while cooking.

To eat, guests use fondue forks or bamboo skewers to spear pieces of the meat; they will cook meat in the broth about one minute. Eat with sauces.

Cucumber Salad

    3 medium-size cucumbers
    2 tablespoons salt
1½ quarts ice water
    1 sweet red onion
    2 tablespoons salad oil
    2 tablespoons vinegar
freshly ground pepper to taste

Slice cucumbers (leave peels on if cucumbers are not waxed), using a potato peeler so that cucumbers are very thin, cutting diagonally making oval-shaped slices. Soak in salted ice water for about 1 hour. Drain. Peel onion, slice thinly, separate into rings; toss with the cucumber slices. Sprinkle salad oil and vinegar over along with freshly ground pepper. Toss until well mixed. Serve immediately. Makes about 6 servings.

Red Sauce

1 cup tomato catsup
2 tablespoons chopped fresh parsley
2 tablespoons fresh lemon juice
1 teaspoon angostura bitters

Blend all ingredients together well and chill. Makes about 1¼ cups sauce.

Fluffy Rice (see index)

Sesame Sauce

1 cup sesame seeds, toasted
½ cup salad oil
1 small clove garlic
½ cup Japanese style soy sauce
2 tablespoons wine vinegar
¾ cup beef broth

Put sesame seeds into a blender and grind until fine and slightly pasty. Add the salad oil and garlic with blender going at low speed. Blend in the soy sauce, vinegar, and broth. Makes about 2 cups sauce.

Bananas in Silk Thread

This is a delightful way to serve bananas. However, you really should prepare them *just* before serving so that the caramelized sugar coating is crisp when they're served. So, before you sit down to eat, have bananas coated with melted butter in one small frying pan (no heat), and have the water-sugar-vinegar mixture in saucepan ready to boil. Have a bowl of ice in the freezer to which you'll add water when you get ready to prepare the dessert. As hostess-cook, you'll have to see that a roaring conversation is going on at the table while you slip into the kitchen to do this.

> 4 *large bananas or 5 smaller ones, not too ripe*
> 4 *tablespoons butter or salad oil*
> 2 *cups sugar*
> 1½ *cups water*
> ½ *tablespoon vinegar*
> *ice water*

Peel bananas, cut in half lengthwise and in half crosswise. Heat butter in frying pan and toss bananas in the butter to coat all sides evenly. (Have this much done ahead before you sit down to eat, if you wish, though it actually doesn't take much time to do.) In a saucepan combine the sugar, water, and vinegar and bring to a rolling boil. Boil, stirring until the mixture spins a thread when poured out of the side of the stirring spoon (310° on candy thermometer). The mixture will caramelize just lightly. Remove from heat and immediately dip the banana pieces into the syrup, one at a time, plunging each sugar-coated banana piece into the ice water as soon as it is coated. You'll have to use your hands to remove the bananas from the ice water; they'll be all crackly and pretty. Drain them on paper toweling and place on serving platter. Makes 6 servings.

Fortune Cookies

Here's another thing to make that requires a bit of coordination and an exercise in timing. If you like that sort of thing (I love making these), you'll have fun making fortune cookies. It's even more fun to dream up the fortunes to put inside. Just type them on little strips of parchment paper and roll or fold up to fit into the cookies.

> ⅔ *cup sifted flour*
> *dash salt*
> 4 *teaspoons cornstarch*

¼ *cup sugar*
5 *tablespoons salad oil*
2 *egg whites*
2 *tablespoons water*

Sift flour and measure, sift again with the salt, cornstarch, and sugar into mixing bowl. Add the salad oil, egg whites, and water and stir until blended. Cover a cooky sheet with foil and drop one tablespoonful of batter for each cooky, baking no more than 6 cookies at one time. Spread batter out to make a circle about 4 inches in diameter. Bake in 300° oven for 20 minutes or until lightly browned.

Remove one cooky at a time from the oven, using a pancake turner. Fold cooky in half, placing fortune inside, then draw ends of the half backward to form a half moon shape and drape over the edge of a pan to crease the cooky. Place in cups or muffin tins to cool so that the cooky maintains its shape. Store completely cooled cookies in an airtight container. Makes 1 dozen.

An Antipasto Fondue Party for After the Game

❂ Outings and games seem to call for a party afterward. Too often we miss the opportunity because we're just stumped for "what to serve." An Antipasto Fondue is the real answer for a mixture of people and an informal time. Serving these tidbits fondue style not only gives people a chance to talk and exchange ideas while their food is cooking, but it allows for flexibility in the amounts that people will eat, too. Some people will be hungry and some will not. This menu will serve 12 persons.

✿

Antipasto Fondue

Tomato Hollandaise   Lemon-Butter Sauce

Hot Mustard Sauce

Chianti   Beer

Coffee   Orange Date Cake

✿

To prepare for the party all you need do is defrost and dry the frozen items called for in the fondue; drain and dry other items. Prepare the sauces ahead of time, and make the cake.

Antipasto Fondue

1 package (12) frozen sausage and cheese pizza rolls, thawed
1 package (12) frozen pepperoni and cheese pizza rolls, thawed
1 package (12) frozen shrimp and cheese pizza rolls, thawed
1 package (6- to 7-ounce size) frozen breaded shrimp, thawed
1 package (about 9-ounce size) frozen potato puffs, thawed
1 package (6- to 7-ounce) frozen crab puffs, thawed
2 cups cooking oil
1 teaspoon salt

Thaw all items, but don't let them stand at room temperature before serving; once thawed, they should be refrigerated. Better yet, thaw them in the refrigerator. At serving time, put all items on a tray, heat cooking oil (add salt to prevent splattering) to 375° in the kitchen. Transfer to lighted fondue burner at the table. Guests spear food items with bamboo skewers or fondue forks and dip in a selection of sauces before eating.

Tomato Hollandaise

3 egg yolks
¼ teaspoon salt
dash cayenne
1 tablespoon tomato paste
½ cup butter
3 tablespoons hot water

Put egg yolks, salt, cayenne, and tomato paste into blender and whirl until smooth. Melt butter and add to the egg yolk mixture with blender going at high speed, blending until thick. Add the hot water as needed to keep the hollandaise pourable. Turn into a small bowl. Makes about 1¼ cups.

Lemon Butter Sauce

¼ cup butter, melted
4 tablespoons fresh lemon juice
dash cayenne

Blend the melted butter and lemon juice together; if you do this in the blender they will remain suspended longer. Mixture will be very thin. Top with a dash of cayenne. Keep hot over candle warmer. Dip shrimp into this. Makes ½ cup sauce.

Hot Mustard Sauce

4 tablespoons dry mustard
1 tablespoon cornstarch
1 teaspoon sugar
1 teaspoon salt
4 tablespoons hot water

Blend the mustard, cornstarch, sugar, and salt together well. Stir in the hot water until mixture is smooth. Use as dip for the pizza rolls. This is *hot*. Makes about ¼ cup.

Orange Date Cake

1 cup butter
1 cup sugar
2 eggs
grated rind 2 oranges
1 cup sour milk, buttermilk, or sweet milk mixed with 1 table-
    spoon vinegar
2½ cups sifted flour
1 teaspoon soda
1 teaspoon baking powder
1 cup dates, chopped
½ cup chopped nuts
Orange Syrup (see below)

Cream butter and sugar together well. Beat in the eggs and the orange rind. Add the sour milk alternately with the flour sifted with the soda and baking powder, mixing until smooth. Fold in the dates and nuts. Turn into a well-buttered 9- by 13-inch cake pan and bake in 350° oven for 45 minutes or until cake springs back when touched in the center. Remove from oven and pour orange syrup over immediately. Makes 12 servings.

Orange Syrup

1 cup sugar
juice of 2 oranges (about ¾ cup)

Bring the sugar and orange juice to a boil and boil for 1 minute. Pour over hot cake immediately. Let juice soak through the cake. Cake may be sprinkled with powdered sugar when cool.

Coffee and Dessert Party Fondue

❉ Dessert fondue is a newcomer on the fondue scene and is ideal for an evening get-together when you've invited people over for coffee and dessert. In the summertime you can enjoy it outdoors—or indoors without heating up the oven. All you need to do is provide the fondue for dipping and the dipping ingredients, which can range anywhere from canned or fresh fruit to cut-up chunks of day-old cake or cookies. For convenience decide on one fondue and serve it with your choice of dippables. If you have an adventurous group, or if your group is as large as ten or twelve, you might want to have two kinds of fondue. We're offering a selection of several fondues here for you to choose from. For dipping, provide chunks of angel cake, pound cake, lady fingers, strawberries, grapes, bananas, papayas, canned mandarin orange slices, pineapple chunks, pitted cherries, etc.

✿

Dessert Fondue
Cake and Fruits
Coffee or White Wine

✿

Preparation of the menu is simple once you've determined which fondue you'll serve. Just arrange the fruits and other dippables attractively on one tray, or pile them into bowls for passing around. Provide small plates and forks or toothpicks. Keep the fondue hot over a very low flame or a candle warmer.

Fondue au Chocolat

9 ounces Swiss milk chocolate, broken into pieces
½ cup whipping cream
2 tablespoons rum

Combine chocolate and whipping cream in top of a double boiler. Heat, stirring frequently, until chocolate melts. If overheated the chocolate can become hard and lumpy, so be extremely careful. Add rum to flavor. Keep warm over candle heat. Makes about 1½ cups fondue, enough for 6 persons.

Butterscotch-Chocolate Fondue

1 cup cream
1 package (6 ounces) semisweet chocolate chips
1 package (6 ounces) butterscotch chips
2 tablespoons butter
1 teaspoon vanilla

Put cream into top of double boiler and heat until warm. Stir in the chocolate chips and butterscotch chips, blending very well and heating carefully so that chips will not harden or melt (overheating causes a failure). Blend in the butter and vanilla. Place over a candle warmer or over very low heat when serving. Makes about 2 cups of fondue, enough for about 8 persons.

Mocha Fondue

½ cup whipping cream
1 pound (16 ounces) milk chocolate (type used for dipping)
1 tablespoon instant coffee
2 tablespoons Kahlúa (coffee-flavored liqueur)
dash cinnamon

Warm cream in top of a double boiler. Add the chocolate, stirring constantly until it is melted. Add coffee, Kahlúa, and cinnamon. Keep warm over low heat or a candle warmer. Makes about 2 cups, enough for about 8 persons.

Nut-Butterscotch Fondue

This one is very sweet, and should be served only to people who appreciate sweets.

⅓ cup light corn syrup
¾ cup well-packed brown sugar
⅓ cup water
4 tablespoons butter
½ teaspoon vanilla
¼ cup heavy cream
1 cup chopped pecans

Cook the syrup, sugar, water, and butter together over low heat until mixture is the consistency of heavy cream. Let cool slightly and add the vanilla and the cream. Stir in the chopped pecans. Serve using a candle warmer or over a very low flame. Makes about 1½ cups sauce.

Quick Fondant Fondue

This one is especially nice with fresh berries.

1 cup unsifted powdered sugar
1 cup heavy cream
1 teaspoon vanilla or 1 tablespoon Cointreau or brandy

Mix powdered sugar and cream in a saucepan. Bring to a boil, stirring; cook for about 30 seconds. Stir in the brandy. Keep warm over very low heat. Makes about 1 cup sauce.

Chilled Golden Custard Fondue

1 package (3 ounces) golden egg custard mix
1⅓ cups milk
1 cup sweetened whipped cream
1 tablespoon orange liqueur, Cointreau, or Triple Sec
1 teaspoon grated fresh orange peel

Prepare custard mix as directed on the package for custard, reducing the amount of milk to 1⅓ cups. Chill until thickened. Stir until smooth. Blend in the whipped cream, orange liqueur, and orange peel. Chill. Makes 2 cups dip mixture. (Note: This fondue is the only one in the whole book that is served chilled.) Dip your choice fruit, cake chunks, and so forth into mixture.

Kaffeeklatsch Fondues

☀ Here's one of the most "fun" kind of things to serve when you've got your friends in for a kaffeeklatsch. The fondues in this group are foolproof and relatively inexpensive to make. You can vary the basic recipe by using different flavored ice cream toppings. If your group is larger than six, you should serve two fondues, simply because it is difficult to get more than six people around one fondue pot. Serve the dunkables in bowls or baskets. People can pick and choose, and even hold to their diet limitations without being noticed. For the chocolate-flavored fondue, it is best to use the type of ice cream topping that comes in a jar rather a can, because you need the thicker consistency here.

❀

Kaffeeklatsch Fondue

Fruits *Marshmallows* *Nuts*
Cake Chunks *Doughnut Chunks*
Coffee or Tea

❀

When you have your fondue ready, set it on a candle warmer to keep it hot enough for dipping. A hotter flame will cause it to burn, and no flame at all will make it get too stiff.

Kaffeeklatsch Chocolate Fudge Fondue

1 jar (10 ounces) fudge ice cream topping
¼ cup whipping cream
2 teaspoons vanilla
fruits, cake chunks, doughnut chunks, etc., for dunking

Heat the ice cream topping and cream over medium heat, stirring constantly. When hot, set over candle warmer. Serve, providing toothpicks or fondue forks for dipping. Makes about 1½ cups.

Kaffeeklatsch Caramel Fondue

1 jar (10 ounces) caramel ice cream topping
¼ cup whipping cream
2 teaspoons rum
fruits, cake chunks, doughnut chunks, marshmallows, etc., for dunking
chopped nuts

Heat caramel topping, whipping cream, and rum together until hot, stirring constantly. Put dunkables into bowls for serving. Provide a bowl of finely chopped nuts. Try dipping fruit, cake, or marshmallows into the fondue, then dip in nuts before eating. Makes about 1½ cups.

Kaffeeklatsch Butterscotch Fondue

1 jar (10 ounces) butterscotch ice cream topping
¼ cup whipping cream
2 teaspoons rum or bourbon
fruits, cake chunks, marshmallows
chopped nuts

Heat topping, whipping cream, and rum or bourbon together to serving temperature, stirring to blend well. Put dunkables into bowls. Put chopped nuts into bowl. Dip fruit, cake, and marshmallows into the fondue, then into nuts. Makes about 1½ cups.

Kaffeeklatsch Strawberry Fondue

1 jar (10 ounces) strawberry preserves
¼ cup Cointreau or orange juice
cream cheese chunks, fresh peach slices, toasted pound cake,
    lady fingers, English muffins, toasted and cut in strips

Heat the preserves and Cointreau or orange juice together until bubbly. Serve over candle warmer with cheese chunks, fruit, pound cake, or English muffin strips arranged on a tray for dipping. Makes about 1½ cups.

Cheesecake Fondue
for a Bridal Shower

What can be more tempting than the flavors of cheesecake and fruit? That's essentially what this dessert fondue tastes like. All the best ingredients of cheesecake are combined to flavor the dipping sauce. You can dip angel cake cubes, pound cake cubes, fresh strawberries—or what have you—into this delightfully flavored fondue. It's so elegant that it's perfect for a special bridal shower, to honor a birthday—anything where something really fine is in order. The group should be no larger than can be seated comfortably around a table. Eight perhaps.

❈

Cheesecake Fondue
Angel Cake Cubes   Pound Cake Cubes   Strawberries
Doux (Sweet) Champagne   Demitasse

❈

To serve this fondue, set the table as "elegantly" as you can, using your best china and linens. Or go completely peasant and set the table with a checkered tablecloth and colorful peasant-like dishes. It's *effect* you're striving for, especially if the party is to honor a very good friend. Make the fondue mixture ahead of time and heat it up just before you're ready to serve it. It needs only the heat of a candle to keep it at serving temperature, so plan to cook and do the reheating in the kitchen before you bring it to the table. Arrange the cake cubes and strawberries on a tray attractively, providing plenty of fresh strawberries (substitute fresh cherries when they're in season). Provide skewers or dessert forks for dipping. Champagne is delightful with this, or you might consider sparkling apple cider or sparkling Catawba juice. When the fondue is about finished, offer the demitasse (or regular coffee if you prefer).

Cheesecake Fondue

½ cup half and half (half milk, half whipping cream)
8 ounces cream cheese
¼ cup sugar
1 teaspoon freshly grated lemon peel
2 teaspoons freshly squeezed lemon juice
1 teaspoon vanilla
dash nutmeg
angel cake cubes, sponge cake cubes, fresh strawberries

Heat the half and half in the cheese fondue pot to simmering. Cut the cream cheese into about ½ inch cubes, and add; stir until blended into cream and completely melted. Add the sugar, lemon peel, lemon juice, and vanilla. Sprinkle with nutmeg. Bring to table and set over a candle warmer. Put the cake cubes and strawberries onto a tray. Provide forks for dipping. Guests spear cake or berries and dip into the cheese mixture. Makes 4 to 6 servings. (You can double or triple this recipe very easily.)

Index